THE REFERENCE SHELF VOLUME 35 NUMBER 6

ITALY

EDITED BY RONALD STEEL

THE H. W. WILSON COMPANY
NEW YORK 1963

THE REFERENCE SHELF

The books in this series reprint articles, excerpts from books, and addresses on current issues, social trends, and other aspects of American life, and occasional surveys of foreign countries. There are six separately bound numbers in each volume, all of which are generally published in the same calendar year. One number is a collection of recent speeches on a variety of subjects; each of the remaining numbers is devoted to a single subject and gives background information and discussion from varying points of view, followed by a comprehensive bibliography.

Subscribers to the current volume receive the books as issued. The subscription rate is $12 ($15 foreign) for a volume of six numbers. The price of single numbers is $3 each.

Library of Congress Catalog Card No. 63-21857

PRINTED IN THE UNITED STATES OF AMERICA

PREFACE

A study of Italy and its people is, in a real sense, a study of the civilization of the Western world. On the shores of this fertile and beautiful land, washed by the Mediterranean and protected by the wall of the Alps, an advanced civilization has flourished for thousands of years. The mysterious Etruscans, the imperial Romans, the martyred Christians, the triumphant Papacy, and finally the contemporary Italian Republic have succeeded one another—each different from the last, but each building on the heritage of the past. A mosaic of history, Italy is the fount of our culture: its legal system is a model for the West, its language is the tongue of music, its Renaissance is one of the great achievements of human endeavor.

Italy, it has been said many times, is an eternal land, a land where the past seems ever-present—whether in the aqueducts built by the ancient Romans, in the wall paintings of the Etruscans, or in the gnarled olive trees that have sustained men for centuries. But Italy is not a museum. On the contrary, it is one of the most vibrant, dynamic, and modern societies in the world today. To visit Italy is to be struck by the ease with which Italians have mastered—and even refined—the principles of the age of mechanization and automation. Italian factories are among the most efficient in the world, Italian design is one of the most esthetic, and the life of Italian society is among the most sophisticated. There is no nation more modern than Italy, none which has its finger more on the pulse of the mid-twentieth century, none which has so well been able to fuse modernism with humanism.

But if Italy has many of the benefits of the modern world, it also has a good many of its problems. Among these are an unstable political system that has resulted in the collapse of nearly thirty different governments since the end of the war; pockets of intense poverty in a nation swept by affluence, but having a potentially dangerous imbalance between the extraordinary riches enjoyed by a few at the top and the relative poverty of the many; a creeping inflation that threatens to take the steam out of the economic boom; a social discontent, a dissatisfaction with the middle-of-the-road government, which has spread among a good proportion—if not most—of Italy's intellectual leaders; and the still-vigorous appeal of communism to Italian voters, of whom one out of every four voted for Communist candidates in the general election of April 1963. Italy today is prosperous (at least in the north) and self-confident (at least on the surface), but serious problems threaten the stability of Italian democracy. Italy, it is well to recall, has existed as a unified nation for only a hundred years. During this century she has twice been swept by war, the first time emerging on the side of the victors and the second time on the side of the vanquished. Under Mussolini's Fascist state, democracy and freedom were unknown for more than twenty years. The Italian Republic, for all its dazzling success, is only two decades old. Its brief history is inspiring, but its future is still far from certain.

The articles in this volume are designed to place the main factors affecting today's Italy into a coherent perspective. The first section sets the framework for an inquiry into Italian problems by recounting key elements of Italy's recent history and by focusing on aspects of the Italian personality and social structure. The second section deals specifically with the Italian political scene and the paradoxical appeal of communism to a nation whose loyalties lie solidly with Western Europe and the United States. The third section is an examination of Italy's booming economy—the *miracolo economico* that has transformed the nation since the war—and the prospects for its future. In the final section the problems of the "other Italy"—the impoverished but slowly changing south—are put under scrutiny.

The editor would like to thank the various authors, publishers, and organizations that have granted permission for the use of materials included in this book.

RONALD STEEL

October 1963

CONTENTS

III. The Economic Miracle

IV. The Mezzogiorno: The Other Italy

ITALY
SWITZERLAND
AUSTRIA
YUGOSLAVIA
FRANCE
ALGERIA
TUNISIA
VAL D'AOSTA
TRENTO-ALTO ADIGE
FRIULI-VENEZIA GIULIA
Trento
Bergamo
Brescia
VENETIA
VENICE
Trieste
MILAN
LOMBARDY
Verona
Padua
Gulf of Venice
Po
Mantua
TURIN
PIEDMONT
Parma
Bologna
EMILIA ROMAGNA
LIGURIA
GENOA
Pisa
FLORENCE
Leghorn
LIGURIAN SEA
THE MARCHES
Siena
TUSCANY
Tiber
UMBRIA
ADRIATIC SEA
CORSICA (France)
VATICAN CITY
ROME
ABRUZZI & MOLISE
LATIUM
PUGLIA
CAMPANIA
Bari
NAPLES
LUCANIA (Basilicata)
Taranto
Brindisi
Eboli
SARDINIA
Gulf of Taranto
TYRRHENIAN SEA
Cagliari
CALABRIA
Strait of Messina
Messina
Reggio
MEDITERRANEAN SEA
Palermo
SICILY
Agrigento
Catania
IONIAN SEA
Syracuse

I. ITALY: ETERNAL AND MODERN

EDITOR'S INTRODUCTION

One of the oldest civilizations in the Western world, Italy is also one of the youngest. The Roman Empire was at its height during the dawn of the Christian era two millenia ago, but the unification of Italy is scarcely a hundred years old. We Americans live under a legal system partially indebted to the ancient Romans, yet the United States of America existed as an independent nation before the states of the Italian peninsula finally achieved unification in the middle of the last century. Italy is old: the memory of the past lives everywhere—in the ruins of the Roman Forum, in the remains of Pompeii and Herculaneum, in the ancient Greek colony of Syracuse, in the walled hill towns of Umbria and Tuscany, and in the splendor of Venice. But Italy is also a young country: young in spirit and in the boundless energy that has made her a pace-setter in art, industry, and fashion. The motor scooter and the typewriter, the skyscraper and the neorealistic cinema, abstract painting and the espresso café bar—these, too, are Italian. The most modern of all countries, and yet one of the oldest: this is the paradox of Italy—the source of her mystery and eternal fascination.

The articles in this first section are meant as a composite sketch of Italian society and the Italian personality. John Ciardi, an American of Italian descent who is both poet and teacher, tries to explain the strange intoxication so many foreigners feel when they come into contact with Italy. In the second article, Joseph Harrison of the *Christian Science Monitor* explores the extraordinary recovery of Italy after World War II. The well-known historian H. Stuart Hughes puts the past half century of Italian history into perspective, while the following article describes the political situation in Italy in the early postwar years. Joan Marble Cook, an American journalist living in Rome, explodes some myths about Italian life, while in the final article of this section, the critic Raymond Rosenthal describes, rather more optimistically, the effect of the triumphal entry of Italy's writers and artists into the modern world.

ETERNAL ITALY[1]

Everything that is most characteristic of Italy certainly begins with the fact that the still-smoldering volcanos that largely formed the land made it a peninsula—a region attached to Europe but fenced off by mountains that have always been enough of a barrier to enforce a difference. The traveler climbing those mountains from the north and west is climbing out of Europe. When he starts down the other side, he is descending into the difference that is Italy.

The first difference he cannot help but feel is in the land itself. The upheaval that formed the land left the bones of rock everywhere visible, softened here and there by erosion and by centuries of incredible toil, and punctuated by dramatic cypresses, but always primordial; pocketed by rich valleys and plains, but always ringed by crags and impoverished slopes at whose feet roar the dangerous Italian rivers, two parts mud to one part water.

The backbone of that geological display is the Apennines, which, broken at the Straits of Messina, rise again to form Sicily, the Italy south of Italy. Built on that mountain spine, Italy is a harsh land, bony and masculine, but all about its shores there dances that incredible blue female sea waving its mists and spangles; while over the rocks themselves, though it be no more than cactus and scrub, the Italian vegetation, its "several greens exultantly specific," as Peter Viereck put it, flames toward that particular Italian sun.

It is a dramatic landscape, its beauties forever poured forth upon the harshness of its stones. Perhaps it is that sense of contrasts that unfailingly overpowers the visitor. "A sight to stir the coldest nature and make a sympathetic one drunk with ecstasy," wrote Mark Twain in September of 1892, describing a sunset over Florence. And though he was no hand at easy ecstasies, that sense of rapture was still powerfully with him a month later, when he wrote, "Late in the afternoon friends come out from the city and drink tea in the open air, and tell what is happening in the world, and when the great sun sinks down

[1] From "The Sense of Rapture," by John Ciardi, poet, former professor of English, and poetry editor of the *Saturday Review*. *Saturday Review*. 44:20-3+. F. 11, '61. Reprinted by permission.

upon Florence and the daily miracle begins, they hold their breaths and look. It is not a time for talk."

Italy is a land to turn any visitor voluble, but always, too, it brings him to his speechless hour. Then suddenly it is as if he heard the wings of time beating above him; as if the past cried "you, too" at the same instant that the present cried "now." There comes upon him, then, a sudden sense of life. "It is impossible to describe the scene," wrote Hippolyte Taine in 1865, repeating a phrase that has long been standard on postcards from Italy. And he added, "Let us open our eyes and live, for we have the flower of life in a glance."

Twain was writing from Florence and Taine from Naples. The two scenes could hardly be more different. Yet it is characteristic of Italy that scenes so different in themselves should both be typically Italian, and both call forth that same rapturous sense of life. The daily miracle waits everywhere in Italy. All clocks stop for it, and all calendars rumple out of sequence.

For the difference that begins as one descends the Alps into Italy is not only of space, but of time. From, say, the Austrian border to Puglia (the heel of the boot) to Lucania (the instep), to Calabria (the toe), or to Sicily, it is roughly seven hundred miles as the airlines fly, and more nearly one thousand as any known road winds. And every hundred miles carries the traveler at least a century back from whatever time he left at the border. Italy, he will discover, is a time machine.

As a matter of accuracy within fantasy, the progression is not an even one. In Milan the traveler can still think of himself as being in the twentieth century. In Florence he simply cannot tell what time it is: time seems to have folded into itself like a pack of cards, the past and present all shuffled together. In Rome he knows the twentieth century is somewhere around because the Romans build monuments to it, though they have never quite learned how to live in them. But by the time he has traveled from Rome to Naples, and then from Naples south, there can be no doubt left in him: he has entered the past. Somewhere a bit south of Rome, he knows he has left his century, the Christian world, and the advertised standard of living. He has entered antiquity, the pagan thicket, and the heartland of that crushing and hopeless poverty the Italians call *la miseria,* and from which they are forever ready to recoil into an exuberance called *festa.*

So separated from time, it is inevitable that he should feel detached from world and care. That feeling of detachment is deeply involved with the sense of rapture. Note again how Mark Twain put it: "friends come out . . . and tell what is happening in the world." Not what is happening, but what is happening out there in some place else that is called, or used to be called, "the world," a place and an existence far outside the time machine.

Perhaps only magic will explain it. If so, Italy has a magic power to divide a man from his life, and thereby to quicken his sense of it. The conventions, the compulsions, the habituations by which one has lived before, seem to be instantly challenged and instantly overthrown. "I scarcely recognize myself or my own spirits," wrote Elizabeth Barrett Browning from Florence in 1847, "all is so different!"

But different from what? Not different from oneself, certainly. One seems to feel rather that he has never been more truly himself. What one feels different from, rather, is the self he had thought he was in that other place called the world. It is a sense of having shed a blindness to walk in the light of a new awareness.

That sense of emergence into a new light is always an intoxicating experience, and the Italians have long since grown used to the tourists' intoxication—grown used to it and built an economy around it. "Send a bookkeeper to Italy and he turns poet," an Italian friend once remarked after dinner; "send a poet to Italy and he turns madman." . . .

Though both my father and mother emigrated from Italy in their teens, I did not have my first experience of it until I was almost thirty-five and on a sabbatical year from Harvard. The year was a sort of second honeymoon for my wife and me, and if that were not enough, our first Italian city, coming down as we had from Salzburg, was Venice. I was instantly dizzy with it. There simply could be no such city on earth: we were clearly on Mars or in heaven or in some marriage of fantasies. In a euphoric outpouring I wrote my mother that she must have been mad to have left such a country. Her answer was a clear capsule.

"Dear son," it read, "I did not have American dollars when I was there."

I thought of her answer again when I read Henry James's account of a stroll outside Florence on a bright afternoon in 1877. He had climbed a hill, light of heart and heavy of pocket, and had come to an unidentified villa with a large view of the countryside. "What a tranquil and contented life it seems," he wrote, "with romantic beauty as part of its daily texture."

James was the tourist born. Not for him the burden of hopeless poverty. Nor the experience, so often reported by emigrants, of returning to Italy at forty or fifty to find that their childhood companions are no longer contemporaries but broken, toothless, old men. The tourist sees the barefoot waifs and thinks how enormous and beautiful their eyes are. He sees the old women bent in perpetual black, like untidy nuns, and thinks how picturesque it is. He sees the peasant battering his rocky soil with his antique and back-breaking tools, and thinks how blessed it must be to live so close to the root of things. Deprivation is nothing to him: let it show . . . [its] face and he reaches for his camera.

Yet, whatever he misses there inside his detachment, what he does see rushes to him with a sense of the first things of his life. His emotions, like his pocketbook, are there on a favorable rate of exchange. He can indulge himself in the presence of the grieving stones of Italy and somehow be moved by a pathos that could even be real; as Charles Eliot Norton was in the presence of Siena, of which he wrote with more self-rapture than real compassion: "This old town which has seen so much bloodshed . . . to so little purpose . . . where the passions of men have burned so hot, and where life has been so full of hazard and adventure."

For that matter, why should he have felt compassion? In Italy, even present grief seems far, and long past. And always there is that equal sense that glorious things, too, have stirred in those stones. "Enough remains of ruined splendor to convince the spectator of all that has departed." The words are Hawthorne's, from "The Italian Notebook," and they refer specifically to the Sistine Chapel, but they could have been spoken of almost any city in Italy. The past stirs full there.

Many a man, in fact, standing in the presence of time, has been filled with a powerful sensation of *déjà vu.* One arrives for the first time and instantly has the feeling that he has been there before; that he has, in fact, been there forever.

Often—especially among the more literate and the more learned—that feeling is preceded by a rapture of anticipation. So Edward Gibbon testified of his first visit to Rome in 1764:

> I can neither forget nor express the strong emotions which agitated my mind as I first approached and entered the eternal city. After a sleepless night I trod, with lofty step, the ruins of the Forum; each memorable spot where Romulus stood, or Tully spoke, or Caesar fell, was at once present to my eye; and several days of intoxication were lost, or enjoyed, before I could descend to a cool and minute investigation.

Twenty-two years later, approaching the city by the same route, Goethe felt the same feeling even more strongly. "My anxiety to reach Rome was so great that . . . even in Florence I stayed only three hours." And if the joy of his first discoveries was less learnedly detailed than were Gibbon's, his account gives an even more immediate sense of reaching a place to which his life had long since traveled. "All the dreams of my youth," he wrote, "I now beheld realized before me; the subjects of the first engravings I ever remember seeing (several views of Rome hung in the ante-room of my father's house) stood bodily before my sight."

It is not hard to account for that special sense that Italy is, from the first, a place returned to. Certainly if a Western man has a mind, it has been to Italy before him. Perhaps he had forgotten to what monuments has schoolhouse was addressed; as he may have forgotten what assumptions, long since native to his way of thinking and being, first entered the civilized mind in sight of these stones. But in Italy he stands in one of the schoolhouses of the world: the minute he enters, he knows he has entered one of the home places of his mind. He has entered not only the landscape of a legend, but of his own legend. The difference he has come to is himself; and somehow he had never understood time, and himself in time, as he seems to understand it now.

It is that exhilarated rush of time upon him, certainly, that has given the Italian his particular genius, the visitor his sense of rapture, and visiting artists the special burst of creativity that inevitably breaks from them in Italy. But if that sense of the rush of time is powerfully of life, it is as powerfully of death.

For in Italy it is no paradox that the principal industry is life and the principal product death. The Italian, as Salvatore Quasimodo once said, has a cult of death. It has been bred into him by everything Americans most readily forget. Life has been cheap there. The very graves are so crowded that it is still the necessary custom to disinter and pile up the bones every so many years in order to make room for the new dead.

In Italy, moreover, things tend not to change. The Italian is still likely to be born in an immemorial stone room in the same bed in which his fathers as far back as memory reaches were born, and in which, if they managed to escape disaster, they died. The Italian has his beginning and his end in the same place. He lives in the very stones that will be his tomb.

And who can estimate the force the Church has been upon him in his cult of death? Where but in Italy could there be such a church as Santa Maria della Concezione (the church of the Capuchin monks) on the Via Veneto in Rome, whose funeral vault is intricately decorated with the bones of over 4,000 monks? . . .

To be in Italy is many things, but always it is to find oneself walking that crypt, or its equivalent, and then to climb back into the sun, into *that* sun. And once up from that boneyard what choice has one but to put on his own death's-head, or to fling his hat in the air and dance? The visitor may undergo a kind of shock treatment in the boneheap of the Italian presence. But always the adjustment comes fast. Up goes the hat in the air. The more death is visible, the more urgent it becomes to live. That news of death is, after all, what one has always known. To have it so dramatized may at first be painful. But listen: there is music in the streets. It's a *festa.* Let's go! There will be time enough to lie dead. But *feel* that sun! What was it Hippolyte Taine said? "Let us open our eyes and live, for we have the flower of life in a glance." The daily miracle is around the corner.

ITALIAN SUCCESS STORY [2]

Nations, like persons, are sometimes inclined to pay more attention to those friends and acquaintances who cause them occasional trouble than to those who do not. Quiet friends do not always receive the full measure of appreciation which is their due.

In the postwar period Italy has been, at least so far as the United States is concerned, one of those quiet friends. While it would be most incorrect to say that Italy has not been appreciated in Washington, one can say that, because of Italy's diplomatic stability, that country has not always received the same publicity or the same attention as have some of its more diplomatically rambunctious neighbors.

Yet, by almost any standards, Italy deserves to have attention focused on its postwar achievements, which have been remarkable in many fields. Its economic growth has been spectacular. Its artistic accomplishments have been unexcelled. Its efforts on behalf of European and Western unity have been unwavering. Its adherence to the democratic way of life, despite many difficulties, has been steadfast.

Although Italians, with their Latin bent for self-scrutiny, may still find a great deal in their country over which to complain, it is only justice to record that viewed from a distance Italy has been on the whole a helpful and hopeful factor in Western affairs.

Those who have made a close study of postwar Italy generally agree that Italian achievements can be traced to one basic fact—the healthy state of mind with which Italy faced up to the mountain of problems which confronted it at the end of World War II. Shackled for two decades with an oppressive and antidemocratic political system, its territory bitterly fought over, crowded with refugees, weakened by severe monetary inflation, much of its industry destroyed, stripped of its overseas empire as well as certain portions of the homeland along its northern frontiers, Italy might well have been expected to sink into a mire of self-pity, discouragement, and resentment.

The overwhelming majority of the Italian people experienced none of these sensations. Instead, the record shows that the average Italian, long known as one of the most willing workers in

[2] From "Italy: a Quiet Success," by Joseph G. Harrison, overseas news editor, *The Christian Science Monitor. The Christian Science Monitor* (Eastern edition). p 13. Mr. 23, '61. Reprinted by permission.

Europe, went to work where he could. He began repairing roads, rebuilding factories, restoring run-down farms. Gradually the nation's economic life began to strengthen itself; more and more goods appeared in shops; the war-created hordes of homeless beggars began to dwindle, and national self-confidence deepened.

No claim is made that Italy was unique in this. Other war-ravaged lands also worked day and night as best they might and showed remarkable results. Indeed, Western Europe as a whole set a record—perhaps matchless—for reconstruction and advance during the decade and half which followed V-E Day.

Yet, in many ways, the Italian achievement was the most surprising. Burdened with the largest Communist party outside the Soviet Union and one which was dedicated to halting progress rather than helping it, endowed with few natural resources, heavily overpopulated, many observers seriously questioned the Italians' ability simultaneously to reestablish democracy and to reinstitute economic progress. Although Italy has suffered from many a mistake and although there are Italians who assert that the nation's forward march could and should have been even swifter, unbiased opinion seems generally to hold that Italy's postwar progress has been outstanding.

It can be said that the nation as a whole, with a certain earthy hard-headedness, took sober stock of the situation in which it found itself and determined to move forward as rapidly as hard, back-bending work and native ingenuity could take it.

Furthermore, the return to democracy apparently released many of those talents which the Italian people have in such generous quantity and which they had not been able adequately to utilize during fascism.

One has but to think of Italian motion pictures and Italian fashions—in both of which categories Italy immediately jumped into the world lead in the early postwar period—to recognize the artistic contribution which this country has made during the past fifteen years.

Italian achievement in both of these fields is considered to be particularly significant in what was revealed of Italian thinking. For while Italy's cinematic successes were due to its ability to analyze and depict human conditions with an unmatched clarity, its fashion success was, couturiers say, traceable to a willingness to break with tradition, to experiment boldly with colors, patterns, designs, and to sense what women around the world were waiting for.

Taken together, this means that Italy was prepared to think sharply and to act forcefully—an excellent recipe for success as well as a good frame of mind in which to confront the mountainous problems of national reconstruction.

While Italian accomplishments in the movies and in fashion may be more immediately eye-catching than its achievements in other walks of life, these latter are equally great and, in the long run, more important. This becomes evident the moment one examines the figures for Italian industrial production upon which the economic well-being of a modern nation so largely depends....

Considering only the year 1960, the gross national product rose by nearly 8 per cent, while gross industrial production went up by the startling figure of some 14 per cent. Economists look upon this latter achievement as remarkable, given the fact that it followed upon the heels of a number of other years in which record after record had fallen.

The over-all picture would have been still brighter had it not been for the fact that . . . [in] many ways agriculture remains the weakest link in the Italian economy, the one in which the least progress has been made and the one which offers the greatest challenge in the future.

A major reason for this is that so much of Italy's farm output is concentrated in the poverty-stricken provinces of the south, where social and geographical conditions have for centuries conspired against progress and well-being.

Yet it is symptomatic of Italy's swift emergence as an industrial power that agriculture now accounts for only one fifth of that country's national income, despite the fact that non-Italian opinion still tends incorrectly to think of Italy largely in terms of a peasant-oriented economy. . . .

Although Italy has been forced—and will continue to be forced for the foreseeable future—to concentrate primarily on internal development, Rome has nonetheless been playing a significant, and on the whole constructive, role in certain important international questions. As distinct from the days of Mussolini, when Italy's role was a clamorous one, these activities of the various postwar governments have been conducted with an almost self-effacing lack of fanfare.

Foremost among these activities have been the following:

1. An unwavering adherence to the ideal of creating a Western European union, which would tighten economic and diplomatic cooperation among the democratic states on the Continent. Although the first impetus toward Western European unity is generally credited to the French, no other nation has been more desirous of seeing such unity achieved than Italy.

Furthermore, the Italian view of European unity has been essentially a broad and generous one. Although a member of the European Common Market (known as the "Inner Six" or "the Six"), Italy has ranged itself on the side of those nations which take the "big Europe" view and would like to see a closer tie with the countries of the European Free Trade Association (also known as the "Outer Seven") led by Great Britain.

2. Whereas for approximately a half century prior to the end of World War II Italy fought and sacrificed in an effort to win for itself an African colonial empire, it surrendered its overseas empire with what is universally agreed to have been impeccable good grace. Granted a ten-year trusteeship over Somaliland, it not only made not the slightest effort to prolong its stay there, but it even undertook heavy financial expenditures on behalf of the natives with little likelihood of receiving any substantial national advantages in return.

3. Faced with a troublesome quarrel with Austria over the administration and future of the predominantly German-speaking region of the South Tyrol, Italy has repeatedly offered to submit the question to the International Court of Justice (the World Court). Although Italy argues that it would have strong legal, moral, and diplomatic grounds for rejecting any suggestion that it discuss this question, it states that it is willing to submit the question to the World Court in the interest of European harmony and a peaceful solution of international disagreements. Austria has not, as yet, agreed.

4. Without pressure from Washington Italy has recently made a number of trade concessions which were a major contribution toward helping solve the present dollar plight of the United States. These concessions were largely in the form of a relaxation of import restrictions against competitive American goods. . . .

Few European governments have shown a greater understanding of the international load which the United States has borne during the past decade and a half. Italy is one of the few nations which has not indulged in the luxury of at one moment expressing gratitude for United States aid and in the next emphasizing America's diplomatic shortcomings. While such Italian consideration may not last forever, there can be little doubt but that Washington has been and is grateful for this restraint.

Actually, no one who followed closely the attitude of the Italian people as a whole during World War II need be surprised that Italy emerged from that conflict in what may be described as a constructive frame of mind. For one of the things which most pleased Italy's friends throughout the Western world was the fact that at no time during that conflict did any large numbers of Italians—incorporated willy-nilly by the Duce into the Axis—surrender their basically civilized frame of mind.

Both during the conflict and immediately after it, the average Italian showed nothing but kindness to the hundreds of thousands of oppressed individuals of all races with whom they came into contact. Although Mussolini urged the Italians to live like lions, with great good sense and fundamental decency the latter showed a strong preference for living like civilized human beings.

What this seems to mean is that few nations have ever been less changed in their fundamental outlook than Italy was by its more than two decades of fascism. Thus Italy was mentally prepared to move forward once the opportunity presented itself with the end of hostilities.

None of this means, obviously, that Italy does not face tremendous problems, that it has not made serious mistakes, that it could not have contributed even more.

There are still extremely grave social and economic injustices in Italy which must be corrected for the sake of both national morality and internal stability. The country still finds some 40 per cent of the electorate voting either outright for the Communist party or for the Left-wing Socialists, who are in working alliance with the Communists. Political democracy still is a plant which needs much watering and care there.

Thoughtful Italians, while pointing out that the same can be said of most other countries, admit the truth of all this. Indeed, the most forthright critics of things Italian are, as they should be, found within Italy itself.

Yet, in the final analysis, the overwhelming bulk of the evidence points to continued Italian progress. Thus the nation, which for the decade and a half prior to the outbreak of World War II was one of the most disturbing factors in international affairs, has during the decade and a half which has followed that conflict been one of the more stabilizing factors on the international scene.

THE PUZZLE OF ITALIAN HISTORY [3]

Most educated Americans think they know something about Italy. Its arts and its tourist attractions are familiar; its language does not seem very difficult; its people welcome the foreigner as a friend. In fact, the apparent ease of acquaintance is deceptive. In some ways we know less about Italy than our fathers and grandfathers did. While many have a traveler's working knowledge of its language, few read its literature in the original; still fewer have followed the sinuosities of its history; the reporting of Italian affairs in the American press has, on balance, diminished in the past decade, and much of what reporting there is, is biased and misleading.

Contemporary Italy's history puzzles us because it seems like an anticlimax. A hundred years ago the bulk of the country was united into the Kingdom of Italy; the hopes of Dante—the longings of seven centuries of Italians for unity and freedom—were apparently fulfilled. The tendency of foreigners was to close the book of Italian history, as with the traditional last lines of a fairy tale: "They lived happily ever after." The Italians, it seemed, had solved their problems: the millennium had come. In fact, the country's confrontation with its true problems, the most significant phase of its modern history, had only begun.

There is a further source of puzzlement. In the past century Italy has led a double history—indeed, it has led a double history in two different senses. Two great contrasts have split Italian life. Two diverging lines of experience have shown how fragile was the apparent national unity achieved in 1861.

The first concerned ideals and political loyalties. When Rome finally became the capital of United Italy in 1870, it had already

[3] From "The Puzzle of History," by H. Stuart Hughes, professor of history, Harvard University. *Saturday Review*. 44:26-8. F. 11, '61. Reprinted by permission.

been another kind of capital for almost two millennia. As the residence of the Pope and the seat of Catholic Christendom, it had possessed an international importance overshadowing that of the capitals of the individual Italian states. The Kingdom of Italy took Rome from the Pope by force; for two generations Pius IX and his successors refused to accept the loss of their territorial dominion. During more than half the history of United Italy, the "Roman question" poisoned relations between Church and state and tormented the consciences of Italian Catholics. As Italian citizens they owed *national* allegiance to a kingdom that was in a state of political warfare with the authority to which they owed *spiritual* allegiance; not until the early years of the twentieth century were good Catholics permitted to vote in Italian national elections.

The agreement of 1929 between Mussolini and Pope Pius XI apparently settled the Roman question. By the statesmanlike compromise of giving the Papacy territorial sovereignty over the few acres of Vatican City, the two authorities were able to square the state's insistence on its right to rule all Italy with the Church's equally strong insistence that its head needed a seat of government independent of any national authority. But the settlement of 1929 was less a compromise than it seemed. In fact, it was Mussolini who made most of the concessions. In return for a renunciation by the Pope of territorial claims that had become totally anachronistic, the ruler of Italy granted nearly all the Church demanded in respect to marriage law and a privileged educational position.

Such concessions might seem only natural in a state whose population was overwhelmingly Catholic. The Church since 1929 has enjoyed no more favor from the Italian state—actually less—than it does in such profoundly Catholic countries as Ireland or Portugal. But Italy differs from countries like these in two important respects. First, as the seat of the Papacy, the Italian state is far more subject to direct Church pressure; combining as he does in his own person the headship of the universal Church with that of the Italian Church, the Pope is far more tangibly present in Italian affairs than he is in those of any other country. Second, Italy is less Catholic than it appears. Besides its small minorities of Protestants and Jews, a vast percentage of its population—more particularly among urban workingmen and intellectuals—is only nominally Catholic. Some are at least baptized, married, and buried by the Church; others have no Church connection at all. Anticlericalism and opposition to the priests have always been strong forces in Italian life and Italian politics. For the past century, a constant struggle between clericals and anticlericals has split Italian society. Most of the time, the majority of the country's democrats have been on the anticlerical side.

Hence it has been peculiarly difficult for Italy to find a satisfactory balance in Church-state relations. For the first generation of its history as a United Kingdom, anticlericals were in control, and their intemperate statements embittered a question that demanded a maximum of tact on both sides. In the generation that has passed since the settlement of 1929, clericalism has been in the ascendant.

The second great split in contemporary Italian life has been between rich and poor—or, in geographical terms, between north and south. The *Risorgimento,* the movement of national regeneration that culminated in the unity of the country, was an affair of a privileged few. It was people of means and education who agitated and fought for the creation of United Italy. Most of the poor, the peasants and the urban artisans, stood on the sidelines, watching the great events of the years 1859-61 with dull bewilderment. And in the decades that followed, the majority of the Italian people felt left out of public affairs, strangers to the national consensus. Not until 1913 were the Italians granted something approaching universal manhood suffrage.

Even in a technical sense, then, Italy has known political democracy for less than a half century. Of these five decades, two were passed under the Fascist dictatorship and another was occupied by the world wars. The first Italian experience with democracy was largely confined to the four years of postwar maladjustments and civil disorder from 1918 to 1922. The second experience began with the overthrow of Mussolini in 1943 and has continued to the present day.

Thus the poor of Italy have found reason to incline toward bitter social protest and extremist leadership. They have been skeptical of the ability of democratic politicians to alleviate their lot. It is natural that Italy should have produced the largest Communist party in the Western world, and that for the first decade of its post-Fascist history the main body of its Socialists traveled meekly in the Communist wake.

Within Italy, the south is poorer than the north. This is true of many countries, including our own, but in Italy the gap yawns more profoundly than in any other major Western nation. South of Rome begins the vast area of agrarian misery: here one feels in another world from the industrial bustle of Turin or Milan. And here the pressure of rural overpopulation has been able to find no adequate outlet—ever since the United States, by its quota laws of the early 1920's, cut off the flood of immigrants from southern Italy and Sicily which in the single year preceding the First World War had reached a quarter of a million.

In the past decade, however, southern Italy has at last begun to come to life. The land-reform measures of the years after 1949 have given the peasants a new hope, and the beginnings of industrialization have opened fresh vistas for urban enterprise. The gap between the two parts of the country is still wide—indeed, in some respects, it has increased, since the northern industrial cities have drawn the major profit from the economic boom of the late 1950's. But a trend toward equalization is already in sight. Moreover, from the wider standpoint of Italian poverty, the worst may be over. At a slower pace, it is true, than France or Germany, but still steadily and cumulatively, Italy is becoming a modern, mobile, and consumption-oriented society. One's judgment of this change depends on the direction in which one makes a comparison. If one turns north and compares Italy to France or Germany or Switzerland, then it seems lamentably in the rear. If one turns east and west and brackets Italy with its Mediterranean neighbors it emerges triumphantly in first place.

The central dilemma, then, of contemporary Italy has been to find a regime that would bring these contrasts and these problems into harmony, a regime that would bridge the differences between Catholics and anticlericals, rich and poor, north and south, and provide Italy with the dynamic leadership required for modernizing its economy and society to bring them up to the level of the most advanced nations of the Western world. A large order, certainly. It is no wonder that Italy has never found a regime with which the majority of its citizens have been satisfied.

For the first half century of United Italy's existence the political regime was a liberal parliamentary monarchy. It was liberal in the sense that the liberties of the citizen were guaranteed by the law and the constitution, and parliamentary in that the essentials of power were in the hands of parliament and the ministry responsible to it. But it was definitely not democratic. The suffrage was based on property, and nearly all the workers and peasants were disfranchised.

The complex and shifting pattern of Italian parliamentary politics required a parliamentary organizer of genius to make the system work. The late nineteenth century had seen a succession of these—Cavour, Depretis, and Crispi, to name those of lasting importance. Not until the first decade of the twentieth century, however, did the tradition of parliamentary management reach its ultimate expression. In the person of Giovanni Giolitti, Italy found the greatest majority-monger of them all. Giolitti gave his country freedom combined with order, economic progress, and cautious reform; he gave it the best decade it would know for half a century and even led it on its first steps toward democracy. But for all his qualities and achievements, Giolitti could not grant what Italian youth craved: a new ideal of martial glory and service to the nation. In the matter-of-fact, uninspiring, business-as-usual manner in which he ran the country, Giolitti epitomized the solid strength and the fatal weakness of the Italian parliamentary monarchy.

Hence it was not surprising that after the cruel experience of the First World War—which Italy entered against the will of the majority of its people and which brought it much suffering and little credit or reward—the country was shaken by violent social discord. During the first four postwar years, Italy struggled to make a reality of its new democracy, while militants of the Left and of the Right threatened to tear society apart. At first it seemed that revolutionary socialism, inspired by the example of Bolshevik Russia, would sweep the country. In the end it was a new form of authoritarian conservatism—Mussolini's fascism—that ended the first Italian experiment in democracy.

This second of the three regimes under which United Italy has lived appears in retrospect a step backward from its parliamentary predecessor. The Fascist dictatorship destroyed the liberties that Italians had enjoyed during the six decades between

Cavour and Giolitti, and gave them very little in return. But this is a verdict of hindsight. When fascism was still untried, millions of Italians hoped that Mussolini would go beyond the accomplishments of the parliamentary monarchy—that he would give them a new pride in their nation, and would at length associate the peasants and workers in a broader political consensus. For a few months or years, Italians of good will could still hope that fascism would bring unity.

Their disappointment was cruel. The arbitrary acts of the Fascist dictatorship proved to be not merely emergency measures to deal with a temporary crisis, but a permanent abrogation of liberty. Mussolini's social and economic enactments, far from helping the working classes, in practice strengthened the position of the rich against the poor. Above all, instead of restoring dignity to the nation through a vigorous assertion of its rights abroad, the foreign policy of fascism proved the ruin of Italy. By his conquest of Ethiopia, his intervention on Franco's side in the Spanish Civil War, and his eventual entrance into the Second World War itself, Mussolini forfeited the good will of the French and British and became totally dependent on Nazi Germany. Month by month his followers fell away. When he was finally driven from power, in the summer of 1943, Sicily had been lost, the Italian mainland was about to be invaded, and his people, almost to a man, had turned against him.

The first phase of the Second World War had brought defeat and disgrace to Italy. Its later phases created the people's proudest memory—a revival and heightening of the *Risorgimento* experience—in the achievements of the Italian Resistance. For the last year and a half of the war, the Resistance fighters redeemed the national reputation through the help they gave to the liberating armies of Britain and the United States, and simultaneously prepared the country for a second and more robust experiment in democracy.

Modern Italy's third regime—the government of Christian Democracy—was a direct outgrowth of the wartime Resistance. Its founder, Alcide de Gasperi, had been one of the chiefs of clandestine antifascism, and his own convictions always remained true to the tradition of Italian democracy. The popular strengths of his party likewise stemmed from the Resistance—its republicanism, its belief in liberty, its concern for the laboring poor, and its effort to remain independent of clerical direction. In his seven and a half years of power from 1945 to 1953, De Gasperi made many compromises with the Fascist past. He was indulgent to the corruption and the authoritarian behavior of his subordinates. Yet in his leadership of a party that sought to combine democracy with an assertion of Catholic values—and economic stability with moderate social reform—De Gasperi gave Italy the most broadly based regime that it had yet known, and the one that came closest to associating the mass of the people in the process of government.

Since De Gasperi's retirement, this third effort to unite the Italians—this third approximation of a satisfactory political regime—has shown its less attractive features. Its leadership has been unsure and has changed too often. . . . Successive premiers, all drawn from the same party and representing every tendency within Christian Democracy, have proved themselves incapable of giving the country a clear and consistent direction. The process of economic reform has slowed. Clerical influence has vastly increased, and abuses of authority on the part of subordinate officials have become bolder and less frequently punished. . . .

The popular demonstrations of July [1960] which toppled the Tambroni government . . . were quite incorrectly reported in the American press as primarily, or even exclusively, Communist. In fact, they represented nearly all shades of Italian antifascism; they restored the militant unity of the wartime Resistance. Faced with the threat of a new authoritarianism of the Right, the forces of Italian democracy closed ranks once again.

The result was the formation of a more broadly based government and a restoration of democratic faith within Christian Democracy. More important than this, the events . . . revealed the danger of entrusting the exclusive direction of Italian democracy to a single party. It drew attention to the necessity of a real electoral alternative. Fortunately, since 1956 such an alternative has appeared in the decision of the Italian Socialists to break away from alliance with communism. Today the Socialists have not cut all their links to their former allies; trade union ties, for example, still remain strong. But . . . the Socialists' independence and self-confidence have grown, and they are now in a position either to present the voter with an alternative to Christian Democracy, or, in alliance with the governing party, to offer an "Opening to the Left," a substantial parliamentary majority for a dynamic policy of reform.

EARLY POSTWAR ITALY [4]

Italy, which had asked the Allied invaders for an armistice and declared war on Germany October 13, 1943, had not bargained for another eighteen months of hostilities and occupation. Yet this period . . . [as Muriel Grindrod, a British historian, comments in *The Rebuilding of Italy*] gave Italians

the opportunity for what many of them still regard as their finest hour: the Resistance movement of anti-Fascist Italians against the Germans and remaining Fascists brought out all that was best in them, and afforded a justification for Italy to be regarded as an ally.

Because Italy had acquired the status of a co-belligerent, liberated areas were transferred from the jurisdiction of the United States-British Allied Military Government to the monarchy, but the Italian ministry was under supervisory control of the Allied Commission until February 1945. Persisting resentment against his role in the Fascist regime led King Victor Emmanuel to abdicate in May 1946; the reign of his successor, Crown Prince Umberto, was short-lived. Early in June the Italian people voted in a referendum to replace the monarchy by a republic. The first cabinet under the republic was formed in July 1946 by Alcide de Gasperi, who presided over a coalition which consisted of eight Christian Democrats, four Socialists, four Communists, two Republicans, and one independent. The peace treaty with Italy was signed February 10, 1947, but occupation forces remained in the country because of fear that the massive Italian Communist party might cause serious trouble for the young republic.

The peace treaty was a bitter disappointment to the Italians, who thought their cooperation and the successful fighting of Italian partisans in the north deserved to be better rewarded. The treaty required Italy to cede much of its naval fleet, renounce possession of offensive weapons like submarines and

[4] From "Italian Politics and Elections," by Jeanne Kuebler, staff writer, *Editorial Research Reports*. *Editorial Research Reports*. 1:179-83. Mr. 6, '63. Reprinted by permission.

bombing planes, and limit its army to 250,000 men and its navy and air force to 25,000 men each. The West renounced economic reparations, but Russia insisted on a payment of $100 million; reparations totaling $260 million were stipulated for Albania, Ethiopia, Greece and Yugoslavia.

Territorial and political questions caused the major difficulties. Italy ceded four small frontier areas to France, the Dodecanese Islands to Greece, and the Adriatic islands and most of the territory surrounding the port of Trieste to Yugoslavia. Trieste itself, with a small hinterland, was constituted a free territory to be guaranteed by the United Nations Security Council. Italy was allowed to retain the disputed province of Bolzano on the Austrian frontier, which had been transferred to her after World War I. This territory, with a large German-speaking population, is now incorporated into the autonomous province of Trentino-Alto Adige, but alleged discrimination against the German-speaking population has led to a continuing dispute with Austria. Following a series of terrorist attacks in the area in 1961, the controversy was placed before the United Nations General Assembly and then withdrawn, but it is still far from settled.

The other major territorial problem, that concerning the status of the Free Territory of Trieste, was not resolved until October 1954. Under the final agreement, Italy retained Trieste, an overwhelmingly Italian city regained from Austria in 1919, while much of the territory of Venezia Giulia surrounding the city was incorporated in Yugoslavia.

The drawn-out resistance of the Germans in Italy after the Allies landed in 1943 caused heavy destruction, but the damage was concentrated in the center of the peninsula and in parts of the south. The rapidity of the advance that finally took place in the north, and action of underground forces against the Nazis, preserved much of the industrial plant. Iron and steel capacity was reduced by only 15 per cent, and textile and other manufacturing installations went virtually unscathed. Nevertheless, the over-all task of reconstruction was enormous:

> One quarter of Italy's railroad tracks, over one third of her bridges and one half of her power plants were destroyed; two thirds of the country's highways were rendered unusable. In 1945, her industrial output was less than half of what it had been in 1938. [Clare Boothe Luce, *Foreign Affairs,* January 1961]

In the early postwar period, emphasis was on direct relief aid for the population. Total United Nations Relief and Rehabilitation aid from January 1946 to the program's close in June 1947 amounted to $549.4 million, most of it supplied by the United States. This aid was largely in foodstuffs, primarily wheat.

In the second phase of reconstruction, from 1947 to 1950, inflation was checked and financial stability achieved, while trade and industrial production began to improve. The improvement was assisted by a $100 million loan from the Export-Import Bank obtained by Premier de Gasperi on a January 1947 visit to Washington:

> On a long-term view this visit laid the foundations for the special interest which the United States subsequently took in Italy's welfare; and it is probably not too much to say that Signor de Gasperi's masterly presentation of his country's situation played an important part in convincing the American authorities of the need for continued aid to war-torn European countries after UNRRA [United Nations Relief and Rehabilitation Administration] should come to an end, thus preparing the way for General Marshall's offer of aid in the following June, which Italy was among the first to accept. [Muriel Grindrod, *The Rebuilding of Italy*]

Special interim assistance and Marshall Plan aid extended in the years after 1947 brought total economic aid to $3.5 billion, about $600 million of it in loans, most of which have been repaid. Such aid established the basis for the long-term development of Italy and its recent strong economic growth. The aid program influenced the Italians to set up the Fund for the Development of the South in 1950. Over-all development has been increased by a ten-year plan instituted in 1955.

The punitive provisions of the 1947 peace treaty were soon outdated. Growing Russian hostility toward the West caused Italy's former conquerors to welcome her participation in the free world's multiplying instruments for economic and military cooperation. Italy became a member of the Organization for European Economic Cooperation at its birth early in 1948 and was among the first to urge political unification of Europe. The Italian government circulated a note among OEEC members in October of that year suggesting that the organization be converted into a political entity advised by parliamentary delegations.

In the course of the following decade Italy joined all of the European and international organizations that offered admission. She was a signatory of the North Atlantic Treaty on April 4, 1949, and of the statute of the Council of Europe a month later. Italy's position in NATO was enhanced when all except the Communist signatories of the Italian peace treaty agreed to a request, made in December 1951, to delete the limitations on her armed forces and weapons.

Italy subscribed to other continental groupings as they were formed: the European Coal and Steel Community in 1951; the abortive European Defense Community in 1952; the Western European Union in 1954; and the European Atomic Energy Community and the Common Market in 1957. Admission to the United Nations, repeatedly denied by Soviet vetoes, was finally accomplished in 1955 under the terms of a package deal.

ITALY: MYTHS AND TRUTHS [5]

Italy . . . [in 1962] finished year-long celebrations of her hundredth anniversary as a nation in an unprecedented blaze of popularity. Not since the Renaissance has the star over the Italian peninsula seemed to shine so brightly. . . .

There seems little question that the place which France once held in the hearts of the Anglo-Saxons has now been usurped by Italy. At every turn the would-be traveler is urged to believe the prevailing myths—that the Italian landscape is glorious, the climate is ideal, the food irresistible and those handsome Italians are the most talented and generous people to be found in Christendom.

As a ten-year resident of Rome and one who feels homesick for *la bella Italia* even after an absence of a few months, it behooves me to point out that the claque is getting out of hand. No country could be as wonderful as Italy is now supposed to be. The time has come to tidy up the myths, to face the fact that there are olive pits in the pizzas and traffic jams on the Appian Way. Not only that but the Italian himself, while justly re-

[5] From " 'La Bella Italia'—Myths and Truths," by Joan Marble Cook, an American journalist living in Rome. New York *Times Magazine*. p 40+. F. 18, '62. Copyright by The New York Times. Reprinted by permission.

nowned for his craft, can also, when the occasion warrants, take high marks for craftiness.

One can criticize any nation for similar or more gross defects; but while most countries take care of the job themselves by producing their own native critics, Italy is unique in producing only enthusiasts.

The first question the average Italian asks a foreigner is, "Don't you think Italy is beautiful?" It is asked with such a winning smile that a negative answer would be unthinkable. It would also be inaccurate because no one can deny the beauty of the Renaissance towns or the charms of the lakes or the haunting appeal of Tuscany and Umbria. The thing the Italian forgets to mention is that there is ugliness as well, in the unsightly new slums that are growing up around all the major cities and in the great patches of semi-industrial land that line the Po like an endless series of city dumps.

The Italian seems blind also to the erosion of central Italy, and when he travels he is so busy admiring the sky and the "golden light" that the devastated countryside escapes his notice.

"And now you must see our beaches," he cries. "We have the most beautiful beaches in the world!"

This could well be true, but unfortunately the Italians have just about buried their beaches under a tangle of highways and cabanas and sticky humanity, and it is as difficult to get a toe into the waters of the Tyrrhenian as it is to climb aboard a Roman bus at lunch time. . . .

The Italians maintain a similar, well-blinkered attitude about their climate. If you run into an Italian friend during one of Rome's frequent (not to say continual) winter downpours he will look surprised if you complain about the weather. "Rain?" he will exclaim. "I hadn't noticed. It rains so seldom here." . . .

And the amount of hoop-la generated about the Italian cuisine might lead one to believe that Italy is a land where one can wander for weeks without eating the same meal twice. Let no one be deceived. The Italian cook has poured nearly all of his talent into spaghetti sauces and after that his repertory drops off fast. He can usually offer some kind of durable meat (the standard diet for Italian cattle is stones and cactus plants) and a green vegetable. His soups and salads and cheeses are fine if left to themselves, but his instinct with everything else is to fry it in oil and flavor it with garlic and rock salt. . . .

The Italian's propaganda about his native land is matched only by his propaganda about himself. With missionary skill he has spread abroad the image of the Italian as a charming, happy-go-lucky peasant, hospitable to strangers and talented in all kinds of handicrafts.

This is about as accurate as presenting a Navajo Indian as a "typical American." For, while the Italian peasant is indeed a man of infinite warmth, humor and generosity, he is disappearing and the only time the tourist is likely to see him is from a train window.

The "new Italian" who is emerging has lost much of the gentleness of his peasant ancestors in his struggle to carve a niche for himself in the rigid Italian class system—a system that until recently allowed only two classes, the rich and the very poor. His memories of yesterday's poverty are still fresh, and he is therefore a materialist in a way that no American can fully comprehend.

He knows that money is the thing that matters. He sees this at the level of the petty bureaucrat where a small bribe will get him an export permit or an exemption from the radio tax. And he sees it in the very top ranks of government, where scandals of "privilege" erupt with disconcerting regularity. One week a central runway at the brand new international airport springs wide cracks; another week bridges on the still unfinished "Autostrada del Sole" start toppling down in confused heaps of concrete and corruption.

Still, the middle-class Italian is better off than he was fifteen years ago. The Americanization of Italy has brought him soap powder (by Lever Brothers), cereals in plastic packages and a shiny new refrigerator in his kitchen. He has put away his motorbike for a Fiat automobile.

Unfortunately, in his rush for comfort he has taken some of the more showy trappings of American culture and left the ideals uncrated. He has adopted the business machine and mass production but has forgotten about child labor laws. If you chide him about this he will explain that there are not enough schools anyhow, and if the children didn't work in the shops they would become *delinquente* like the children in America.

Once he has risen above the level of bare subsistence the Italian is able to devote himself to his favorite pastime—keeping up a *bella figura*—a good appearance. He may lounge around his home in an old bathrobe, but when he emerges onto the street he is wearing a well-tailored English tweed suit and his shirt is snowy. He likes to keep his car as well polished as his shoes, and if he is a really dashing type he takes the muffler off the motor and beefs up his horn until it is as scary as an air raid siren.

There are several things that an up-and-coming Italian *signore* will not do. He will not do the household shopping, he will not ride in a car that is driven by a woman, and he absolutely refuses to leave a shop carrying a wrapped paper package. If his wife isn't along to carry it he sends the maid for it, or has the store send it home by messenger.

The Italian's home is his private domain and he likes to keep one *salotto* spick-and-span (and closed tight) to be used only for major ceremonial occasions. Actually these occasions come less frequently than might be expected because the middle-class Italian is so involved with his relatives that he has little time for anyone else. He expects his entire family, including aunts, cousins and assorted grandparents, to join him for two big meals each day, and once dinner is over it is not uncommon for the whole group to go out to a stylish café for coffee.

Italian families also spend long evenings watching television. The problem of stereophonic sound does not exist in Italy because TV owners turn their sets on so loud that they can be heard all over the neighborhood. In the warm weather when the windows are open, Rome sounds like a giant Cinerama theater.

The "new Italian" does not respond with charity to suggestions that he makes too much noise. He tends to look on outsiders, especially policemen, postal workers, street cleaners and tax collectors, with deepest suspicion. On New Year's Eve he takes enormous delight in pitching all his broken crockery and glass out onto the pavements. When a garbage strike occurs, he simply takes his garbage downstairs and hurls it into the gutter, complaining in outraged tones about the Communists in the street-cleaning department.

His attitude about taxes is even more anarchistic, and to watch the game of hide-and-seek between Italian taxpayers and collectors is to watch one of the great dramatic shows of the land. The practice of keeping two sets of books and reporting profits far below actual figures is so widespread that firms who make honest tax reports are at a serious disadvantage. An American poultry firm operating near Naples was nearly taxed out of business until the harassed managers persuaded the tax people that they weren't hiding nine tenths of the profits in the chicken coops.

The *imbroglione* [clever operator] who spends his life watering the wine or diligently pursuing new ways to sidestep the law is a regular adornment of the Italian scene. He achieves his finest bloom in the form of the Roman landlord. Not long ago some American friends rented an apartment in the Via Veneto section of Rome. They discovered after staying in the place a week that the only water was supplied by a janitor who climbed a ladder to the roof and emptied a few buckets of water into their tank.

While the Italian claque is responsible for the myth of the barefoot, happy Italian, the Anglo-Saxon claque must be blamed for the ill-founded reports of a cultural renaissance in Italy—reports that are far more prevalent in New York and London than they are in Milan and Rome.

Even the Italian critics admit that there is a tendency to let things drift culturally today, while harking back to the glory of Dante and Donatello. They point out something all foreigners in Italy know—that Italians simply don't read books. The sight of a woman reading anything but a movie magazine under a hair dryer brings horrified cries of *intelletuale* from the other ladies. A man lying on a beach reading a book in summer is sure to be not Italian but English or American.

Apathy on the literary scene is underlined by the fact that a book has only to sell 4,000 to 8,000 copies in Italy to be considered a best seller. The nation's writers are better known abroad than they are at home.

The Italian people pay a bit more attention to their artists because they are a more colorful crowd and easier to appreciate. It is significant, however, that the moment an Italian artist starts to gain recognition he turns his gaze toward the United States, often moving here if he can.

The artists and critics agree, although not always for the record, that the excitement in modern art now comes from New York. The Italians, says critic Katherine Kuh, are not "inventors" but "gifted followers."

The same situation prevails in music and the theater; there are talented men and women at work but the new renaissance has not arrived. Italians have never been averse to music and drama, but for the present they prefer to pick up rock 'n' roll from the radio and create their dramas on the audience side of the spotlights.

The question arises: if Italy is so difficult, why do thousands of Americans live there in relative contentment and thousands more dream of following them? There are several answers.

The vaunted golden light that bathes *la bella Italia* these days conceals a quantity of counterfeit, but all is not dross that glitters on the Italian boot. Indeed, in two fields—architecture and the cinema—Italians are not only pre-eminent today, but may make a lasting name for themselves during this century.

The Italian architect can still be pretty dim when he is drawing an apartment or a villa, but the verve of his Roman ancestors wells up within him when he designs a big public monument or building. The noted Italian builder, engineer Pier Luigi Nervi, won world-wide acclaim for the buildings he designed for the Olympic Games. . . .

Appropriately, the Italians have achieved their greatest integrity in the art where they have dared to criticize themselves —in films. A series of talented directors have turned their cameras loose to explore the diseases of Italian society. The results are powerful.

Vittorio de Sica has for twenty years been producing brilliant neorealistic films which show not only the weakness but also the warmth of the Latin character. Federico Fellini rescued the sagging film industry a year or so ago with *La Dolce Vita,* his tale of decadence in high places. Luchino Visconti soon followed with *Rocco and His Brothers,* and there are more exciting films to come.

Italy's greatest comic actor, Alberto Sordi, is also deft at baring the foibles of the Italians, whether he is portraying a pompous money-grabber, Benchley style, or that common figure, the Roman lady-killer. Sordi's popularity, in fact, points up one of the saving graces of the Italians. They know better than anyone what their faults are and as long as the criticism is kept inside the family they are willing to be amused.

Laughter is very much a part of the Italian scene, and if a foreigner can break through the language barrier, he can often experience with an Italian a flash of humor, a recognition of the human predicament that is immediate and electric. It is this human contact, this personal immediacy that keeps all Anglo-Saxons returning to Italy again and again.

There are practical considerations as well. Italy is still cheaper by far than America. One can find maids there for less than $50 a month, and skilled artisans abound who will cheerfully scrape down dining-room tables or make leather purses to one's own designs.

But the best thing that Italy has to offer is time. We move back ten or twenty years when we are in Italy, into a slightly less hectic era when men worked with their hands and older customs prevailed. The fishermen still dry their nets on the beaches around Naples and we need drive only a short way into the country to see women threshing grain by hand and drying tomatoes in the warm sun.

There seems to be more time to enjoy living, too. The three-hour lunch has so far resisted the pressures of the machine age, and conversation is a national pastime. Communication between individuals, the striking of a human spark, is still the Italian's truest joy. He may approach us with love or admiration or envy, but never with indifference. We are ready to put up with a great deal to escape indifference.

CULTURE AND THE ITALIANS [6]

It may seem incredible, but Italy, the home of fascism and futurism, has only recently entered the modern world. I know that since the war many observers have been warning of Italy's galloping Americanization, yet their forecasts seemed to me premature. A few juke boxes could hardly be considered the triumph of technological idiocy. Now, however, there can be no doubt that a fatal transition has taken place. I had been away for five years, and when I returned this summer I could

[6] From "Italy and Mass Culture," by Raymond Rosenthal, American literary critic. *New Leader*. 45:24-6. D. 10, '62. Reprinted by permission.

immediately see that in the interim the dirty work had been done. To an American, especially, that muted screech of mechanized frenzy is always unmistakable. So prosperity and social peace have succeeded where social strife and cataclysms failed: Italy's provincial somnolence has finally been disrupted.

My first reaction was vindictive. After all, why shouldn't Italians have the chance to suffer from the benefits of prosperity, like all the rest of us? Why shouldn't they too carry the burden of cars, television sets, expensive, noisy vacations, ready-made clothes, installment buying, housing projects? Why shouldn't they too stage symposiums on the blighting effects of the comic strips? Why shouldn't they too have their humanist critics standing waist-deep in the sewage of popular culture to fish out the neglected jewel for the delectation of the happy few? Why shouldn't they too have their anguished actor-thinkers torn to shreds by a slick but equally anguished producer—thinkers *à la* David Susskind?

No one can deny them these ecstasies, and they shall eventually have them. But things have not yet reached this blissful pass. True modern life, with its morose accompaniment of violence and anonymity, is gathering force for the assault; it has a long way to go before the last Italian individual is submerged in the viscid tide of stereotypes. Play-acting is a favorite Italian pastime, and right now hordes of Italians are intent on play-acting the part of mass-men, complete with transistor radios to disturb their neighbors, disjointed gabble about the latest movie and best seller, and an ever-mounting incidence of automobile accidents to punctuate the holidays. But side by side with them the majority of Italians persist in play-acting the ancient roles: a shoemaker is quintessentially a shoemaker, a government clerk quintessentially a government clerk, a judge quintessentially a judge. Like great bravura actors who have spent a lifetime perfecting their parts, they throng the streets and piazzas, each man so wholly himself that only artistic concentration and care could produce such impeccable performances. The decor of Italian life may finally succumb to the barbarian advance of the real estate sharks and the bull-dozers; each day another precious national monument is chipped at or even carted away; but modernism's battering progress finds a natural limit and dike in the Italian's obstinate self-concern and independence.

You may convince this easy-going fellow that his earthly happiness is not complete without a refrigerator and a car; but you will encounter some difficulty on the more immediate, animal levels. Bread is still bread in Italy, brown and with a crust, not the puffy, airfilled mush that adorns our supermarkets. And the pleasure the Italian gets from voluptuously cutting his own bread will never, at least in our lifetime, be wiped out by mass-production packaging. In Italy the convivial, physical delights die hard. I doubt that Italians, though eager for technology, are ready to exchange their traditional pleasures for the grim stoicism demanded by industrial efficiency. Perversely, they balk at the sacrifice of creature comforts which the Americans offer up every day without so much as a second thought.

I should imagine that this perversity is currently being examined by a committee of experts. In the meantime, until that problem has been solved, the Italians seem to be enjoying a kind of Indian summer of sudden prosperity. Lacerating noises rend the air, produced by all those new mechanical contrivances which the newly moneyed have purchased. But the predominant atmosphere is one of languid, sensual enjoyment. For the moment, the Italians are giving the rigors of modern life their peculiar accent. How long it will last is another question.

In this miraculous transformation, books, together with many other cultural commodities, have suddenly become a recognized appurtenance of all self-respecting middle-class persons. And since Italy has been caught unawares by the cultural wave and has not yet developed its appropriate Herman Wouks and Allen Drurys, the country's best and most serious writers have been called on to fill the gap. Thus, Alberto Moravia, Giorgio Bassani, Carlo Cassola, and Giuseppe di Lampedusa have all had their turn at being best sellers. Since the Counter Reformation, when society and the Church went one way and culture another, this is the first time that Italy's intellectuals and artists have managed to gain their fellow countrymen's attention. It is a great occasion; and also a bewildering one to the literary plughorses who, for almost half a century, have been accustomed to carrying out their esoteric activities in undisturbed semi-privacy. . . .

Indeed, there is a hectic, heady atmosphere in Italy which reminded me of the untrammeled, yearning idealism that characterized the twenties in America. Prosperity killed friendly artistic gregariousness in America, but in Italy, strangely enough, it has had precisely the opposite effect. In Rome, during the summer months, one could see the entire artistic and intellectual colony gathered in one café. And these were not the solemn conclaves that used to unfold in Café Greco's velvet-paneled sanctuary; they were a much more open, rowdier affair, as though these middle-aged writers and artists were taking a last fling at heedless adolescence. Remembering the status struggle back home, I was amused to see famous names in Italian literature crowding every table in indiscriminate proximity to nonentities, eager to talk to anyone who had anything to say. And all this against a chattering backdrop of posh movie people, as if to remind the participants where most of the money was coming from. The spectacle was gay and colorful, but I sensed an undercurrent of troubled uncertainty.

Was this the last huddling together of a superseded creative minority? The final foregathering before the crushing onslaught of tomorrow's mass culture hordes? There is no doubt that in the coming years the cultural battle will become sharper in Italy; places like Café Rosati will be swept away. At the moment, however, prosperity swathes the future enemy camps in a sparkling, sensual haze. The heckling voices are heard only on the fringe of the merriment. Ignazio Silone and Enrico Emanuelli recently attacked the literary log-rolling machine which tends to favor a select few among the nation's writers. But the disconcerting possibility is that tomorrow their novels may be subjected to the same publicity treatment and have the same large sales. Of course, this will not change the situation, which is fluid, confusing and, for the younger writers, vastly inspiriting.

I am thinking of writers like Renzo Rosso, Giovanni Arpino, Elémire Zolla, Giuseppe Cassieri, Ottiero Ottieri and Saverio Strati. All of them have undoubtedly been bedazzled for a moment by the new, glittering flood of money and opportunities, but none of them have loosened their grip on their sense of artistic craft or their combative social instincts. It is wrong to try to label a whole generation; nevertheless, I would say that this artistic generation's prime characteristic is a sort of saddened socialism, the result of the disheartening political events since the war—saddened yet still firmly convinced of the creative potential of the Marxist ethic and critical insight. In any case, some form of Marxism and social concern still provides most of these young men with the backbone and nerve to withstand the mass cultural assault.

Each in his own way has met the challenge: Giovanni Arpino by his series of elegant and moving novels; Renzo Rosso by his long short stories, among which the story entitled "The Bait" sums up the Resistance era in European history as fully and poignantly as Joyce's story, "The Dead," summed up the era of nineteenth century romanticism; and Elémire Zolla, by his brilliant, satiric social essays, "The Eclipse of the Intellectual" and "Vulgarity and Pain," which launch a frontal attack on the foundations of mass culture, condemning it on humanistic grounds that would constitute a revelation to the American critics, who are still busy trying to isolate and channelize the "good" aspects of the mass cultural industry.

I could go on with the list, but that is not the point. The important thing is the ebullience and excitement one feels in the work of these men. Disillusionment with politics has only strengthened their individual desire to probe to the depths of the social evil. In fact, I think that not having political ties has been greeted as a liberation by these young writers.

A recent book, *The Generation of the Difficult Years,* publishes the results of an inquiry among the writers and journalists who came to maturity during and after the war. All their replies reflect that disillusionment with politics and that dismay in the face of advancing mass culture which are dominant moods in Italy's intellectual circles. Ottiero Ottieri's contribution is typical. A young novelist who has written chiefly about the impact of industrial life on Italy's peasant population, he admits that he has less belief in Socialist values than he had a few years back, Why?

> Because [he answers] a writer, even the most *engagé,* is still just a writer and, like many ordinary men, is subject to history's ebb and flow. I can say that in the last years I have been subjected to the eclipse of socialism and social interests. I have been subjected to the recrudescence of the bourgeois Western world, and I think I'm not the only one.
>
> . . . It is impossible to deny that the withdrawal of the possibility of socialism has led to an explosion of vitalism, of avant-gardism, of eclecticism and adventure, etc.; of individualistic, bourgeois values—

especially among the so-called bourgeois intellectuals of the Left, who had suppressed them. What is being born, or reborn, is the idea of success. Let him who is not striving for success throw the first stone. It was not like this ten years ago: success was collective, because it was the victory of a class. Today it is the big circulation magazine and money. And the main subjects are immorality and eroticism. . . . All this happened not because the social problems were solved. We know that much, or all, has remained as before. The new scale of values is more colorful, more alluring and glamorous, more widely spread through every class, even the working class; but it is fragile and at times frivolous and desperate.

Sounds familiar, doesn't it? I also think that it sounds extremely hopeful. These young men know where they stand; they have not dropped their convictions at the first cry of panic or prosperity. Perhaps it is due to Italy's perverse backwardness, but then all I can say is three cheers for backwardness.

II. THE POLITICAL PARADOX

EDITOR'S INTRODUCTION

There is a strange paradox about the Italian political scene. Led by a middle-of-the-road government firmly in the democratic tradition, Italy is a charter member of the Common Market and a loyal participant in the North Atlantic Treaty Organization. At the same time, Italy boasts the largest Communist party in Western Europe. Approximately one Italian voter out of every four consistently casts his ballot for the Communist candidate. At the April 1963 elections, the Communists captured a greater proportion of the votes than they did in the last election of 1958, and increased their strength in the parliament. Yet Italy today is in the full flush of an economic boom—her *miracolo economico* —that has brought unprecedented prosperity to millions of Italians.

Why should one quarter of the voters of a democratic nation cast their ballots for the Communist party? How can people be Catholics—as most Italians are—and Communists too? People are supposed to be tempted by the slogans of communism only if they are miserable and hopeless. But Communist strength is at its greatest in that very area of Italy where the people are the most prosperous—the industrial "Red belt" of the north. Is Italian democracy threatened by revolution from within? Or are Italian Communists—who swear that they will come to power via the ballot box rather than by force—different from those in other nations? Why has the Christian Democratic party, which has ruled Italy since the end of the war, been unable to pass the reforms that would woo voters away from communism? Does the promised "Opening to the Left" spell a new era in Italian politics that will strengthen the forces of democracy? These are some of the questions that the articles in this section explore.

The first article explains the various Italian parties and their place in the nation's political structure. In the next article, Claire Sterling, an American political journalist based in Rome, comments on the manner in which the "lost decades" of Italian history under the rule of Mussolini and the Fascists are ignored. In the following two articles the implications of the April 1963 elections are examined, in particular the strong showing of the Communist party. The next three articles deal with aspects of communism in Italy: Mario Rossi explains its appeal to young voters, Joan Marble Cook discusses its attractions to intellectuals, and Robert Neville deals with the paradox of how a nation can be both Catholic and Communist. In the concluding article C. L. Sulzberger ponders the future of democracy in Italy.

ITALIAN POLITICAL PARTIES [1]

For all its history and cultural traditions, Italy as a nation is much younger than the United States. Some eighty-five years after the birth of a unified state, the present-day republic was established on the ruins left by war and fascism in a country whose economy was at a standstill and whose people were starving.

In the immediate aftermath of defeat, the most urgent political problem facing Italians was to establish the framework for effective democratic government. The task was greatly complicated by a multiplicity of parties, by differences as to whether the monarchy should be retained or abandoned and an understandable cynicism, inherited from the past, on the part of many Italians toward government in general.

In a nation-wide referendum held in 1946 the Italians elected delegates to an assembly to draw up a new constitutions which was to go into effect January 1, 1948. In the same referendum the people were called upon to decide whether to keep the weakened and discredited monarchy or turn to a republic under a president. Some 12.7 million people voted for a republic against 10.7 million (mostly from the south) who still favored a monarchy.

The president is Italy's chief of state, but the prime minister is the more important official. The president is something more

[1] From *Italy—Change and Progress,* pamphlet by Jane Perry Clark Carey, former State Department official and assistant professor of government at Barnard College, and Andrew Galbraith Carey, former chief of the Industry Division (for Italy) of the now defunct Mutual Security Administration. (Headline Series no 158) Foreign Policy Association. 345 East 46th St. New York 17. '63. p 71-2. Reprinted by permission.

than a figurehead, although the lines of his authority are not sharply delineated in the constitution and the concept of the office has changed with its past incumbents—Enrico de Nicola, Luigi Einaudi and Giovanni Gronchi. The present president, seventy-two-year-old Antonio Segni, was chosen by Parliament in the spring of 1962 after a bitter fight, especially within his own Christian Democratic party, over the choice of candidates.

The most important function of the president is to nominate the prime minister, whose official title is President of the Council of Ministers. On the prime minister's recommendation the president nominates the other ministers. The prime minister is responsible for shaping and administering the government's general policy. He and his cabinet are legally responsible to both houses of Parliament, the Chamber of Deputies and the Senate, and must secure a vote of confidence from each chamber within ten days of formation. . . .

[Since the end of World War II, Italy has had more than twenty changes of cabinet.] Superficially it may seem instability is the rule. Yet, except for a few postwar months in 1945, the backbone of all Italian governments has been the Christian Democratic party. Ministers in ousted cabinets frequently appeared in succeeding ones, often holding the same office as before.

Many Italians vote for the Christian Democrats at election time because there is no acceptable alternative. The party itself—the largest and most influential on the Italian political scene—is made up of a wide variety of people with sharply divergent views. Some advocate the same economic reforms urged by Left-wing parties, including nationalization of key industries. Others believe in free enterprise and oppose government control. Christian Democratic support has been recruited chiefly from the upper and middle classes, the women and the countryside. The party has been held together by its Catholicism, general pro-Westernism and a desire to keep the republic from the political extremes of communism or fascism.

In 1948 in the first elections held under the new constitution, the Christian Democrats secured 48.5 per cent of the seats in the Chamber of Deputies and slightly less of the elective seats in the Senate. In that year the economy was still at low ebb, and the danger of communism was so real that the party's cohesion was greater than it has ever been since. In the 1953 parliamentary elections, the party lost ground, securing only 40.08 per cent of the vote for the Chamber. This result was partly due to a new, unpopular electoral law which had been initiated by the Christian Democrats. In 1958, they obtained 42.4 per cent of the vote.

The great leader of the Christian Democratic party, the late Alcide de Gasperi, who died in 1954, served as prime minister in all Italian cabinets from 1945 until 1953, when his government fell and he became secretary of the party. De Gasperi felt it was important to establish as broad a base as possible of party and popular support for the difficult tasks of reconstruction and social reform that faced the nation under the new constitution. Moreover, devout Catholic though he was, he was aware of tendencies toward clericalism within his own party and believed that needed elements of balance would be provided by a coalition government of Christian Democrats with such moderate secular parties as the Social Democrats, Liberals and Republicans. Beginning with the first government formed under the new constitution, he tried various combinations of this quadripartite formula to achieve stable government. A brilliant politician and skilled negotiator, Alcide de Gasperi was generally able to maintain discipline within the coalition and to keep control over his own Christian Democratic party, which at times threatened to veer off Center toward Right or Left or to spit in two. De Gasperi, an ardent advocate of the unity of Europe, was unquestionably the outstanding leader and statesman of international stature produced by Italy in the postwar period. . . .

The Communist party is Italy's second most influential political grouping; it has consistently obtained about a fifth of all votes cast in postwar parliamentary elections. The Communists dominate the country's largest trade union, the Italian General Confederation of Labor (CGIL), and control local government in various municipalities.

In the immediate postwar period, card-carrying party members reached a high of some 2.5 million; today they have declined to about 1.7 million, only a comparatively small number of whom are indoctrinated Marxists of any kind. Communist strength is found among industrial city workers and farm laborers in certain sections of the country—not necessarily the poorest—such as Tuscany and Emilia. The party also has its quota of intellectuals and middle-class members. As for the millions of nonparty members who vote Communist on election day, they do so in protest against unemployment, bad living and working conditions, low wages, or because of cynical disillusionment with other political parties.

The steady decline in party membership since 1945 is an index of communism's diminishing appeal in Italy. This is due in part to the boom in the Italian economy, which is bringing prosperity to wider segments of the population. In part it is due to a growing disaffection among Communists and their sympathizers, which began to manifest itself in the wake of Moscow's suppression of the Hungarian revolution and Nikita S. Khrushchev's revelations of Stalin's crimes.

Doubtless the decline in Italian Communist strength would have been even greater were it not for the skillful leadership of Palmiro Togliatti, who has been at the party's helm for many years. Togliatti returned to Italy in 1944 after a long period of exile in the U.S.S.R. and elsewhere. He served in the first postwar government and in every cabinet but one until 1947, when De Gasperi ousted all Communists and Socialists from government posts. Under Togliatti's leadership the Italian Communist party has been tactically the most flexible and freewheeling of any of the major Western Communist parties. An ardent advocate of peaceful coexistence, Togliatti has warmly backed Khrushchev's policies in international Communist councils.

At the present time, the Italian Communist party constitutes no revolutionary threat to the existing governmental institutions; nor is it likely to in the future, barring some drastic deterioration in the country's economic or political situation. The party has assumed a pose of moderation and has tried to build up its image as a defender of the republic rather than a revolutionary force trying to overthrow it. Communist leaders maintain they wish to come to power by nonrevolutionary parliamentary means and they would like to cooperate with other parties on a broad program of social reform, combined with an anti-NATO and anti-United States foreign policy. At the December 1962 party congress, one informed observer said that the "Red orators all talked like Social Democrats and sometimes Christian Democrats . . . and all even looked very bourgeois."

For much of the postwar period Italian Communists and Socialists worked together in a so-called "unity of action" pact. Since 1956, the ties between the two parties have weakened. The Communists, reacting with considerable alarm to their threatened isolation on the Left, have tried in vain to prevent the Socialists from dissolving the bonds.

Usually at the other extreme from the Communists, but frequently voting with them in opposition to the government, are the Italian Democrats, a coalition of two former Monarchist parties; and the Fascist party, known as the Italian Social Movement. Lacking any coherent philosophy or realistic aims, the Monarchists, formerly strong throughout the south, have been all but abandoned everywhere except in Naples. The party's dominant figure is the shipping magnate, Achille Lauro, who was a long-time mayor of the city. He attempts to lead his party along conservative and reactionary lines by providing free spaghetti and football, if not bread and circuses, to keep Neapolitans in line.

Today, as always, violent and strident nationalism are the distinguishing features of the Fascists. Advocating worn-out shibboleths in an Italy increasingly international in economic and political outlook, the Fascists look back to the so-called social republic improvised in 1943 by Mussolini at Salò in northern Italy. They appeal primarily to the aging, to veterans to whom the memory of Mussolini is still alive, and to a few disgruntled youths. Popular support for the Fascists is small. They hold 4 per cent of the seats in the Chamber of Deputies only because they are able to obtain financial backing from sources ready to oppose the existing government at any cost. Fascists do, however, have considerable power in some cities and provinces. And not a few local governments have been based on coalitions of Christian Democrats, Monarchists and Fascists. In Rome, for example, the city government until 1962 was based on such a coalition because of the considerable strength of ex-Fascist functionaries and military personnel living there and hoping for a return of the dead past. In some localities, Monarchists and Fascists have even cooperated with Socialists and Communists against the Christian Democrats. . . .

Republicans, Social Democrats and Liberals make up the three relatively small but important groupings that share a secular tradition going back to the nineteenth century. The three parties favor constant vigilance to assure separation of Church and state; all three are strongly anti-Communist and pro-Western. . . .

Since 1954, when De Gasperi died, differences among the three parties have grown. The Social Democrats, led by Giuseppe Saragat, have been anxious to achieve a merger with the larger Socialist party from which they split in 1947 because of their opposition to Socialist-Communist cooperation. The Liberals, under the able leadership of Giovanni Malagodi, have become increasingly conservative in their economic views and believe strongly in laissez faire for business. Today, they refuse to join a government coalition that includes Social Democrats.

As the results of prosperity have begun to be felt in such cities as Milan and Turin, the ranks of both the Liberals and Social Democrats have grown. The Liberals have drawn strength from former Monarchists and especially from the Christian Democratic right, which despises the leftward trend within their party; the Social Democrats have attracted Socialists who have prospered and are enjoying a comfortable middle-class existence.

The Socialist party, founded in 1892, is Italy's oldest Marxist party and the third largest today. In the course of its long history it has suffered many splits and has given birth to parties with such radically different orientations as the Communists and Social Democrats. . . .

Pietro Nenni, the Socialist leader, started his political career as a Republican many decades ago, but in 1921 turned to socialism, which he saw as the only effective way of reforming the social order, abolishing war and combating fascism. Exiled during the years of fascism, Nenni returned to Italy in 1943, where he served as deputy prime minister under De Gasperi in the first Italian postwar government and as minister of foreign affairs in 1946. Since his ouster from office in January 1947, he has not held any official government post.

In 1946 Socialists and Communists concluded the abovementioned unity-of-action pact, providing for coordination of decisions. Shortly thereafter, opponents of communism within the Socialist fold broke away and formed the Social Democratic party. Smaller breakaways by other Socialists hostile to their party's close cooperation with the Communists took place subsequently.

From all the evidence it appears that Nenni was never a happy bedfellow of the Communists. After the Hungarian revolution and Khrushchev's denunciation of Stalin in 1956, Nenni became increasingly restive over his party's links with the Communists. Among the Socialists themselves there was mounting opposition to close Socialist-Communist cooperation. Yet it was not easy for Nenni to disengage his party from the unity-of-action pact. Many local governments were dependent on the Socialist-Communist alliance; the Italian General Confederation of Labor, Italy's largest trade union, whose membership was heavily Communist and Socialist, would be adversely affected by a split. Moreover, Communists had infiltrated the Socialist party; its newspaper, *Avanti!*, was in part dependent on Communist funds; and strong forces within the party, including some of its prominent leaders, still favored close cooperation with the Communists.

Slowly, nonetheless, Nenni acquired sufficient control over his party's apparatus. By 1962, if he had not broken definitively with the Communists, he had so loosened the bonds that he was able to offer the Fanfani government "external support" in Parliament, i.e., he agreed to refrain from voting against the government. . . .

As this brief survey of the Italian political scene suggests, the multiplicity of parties in Italy is a major factor contributing to changes of government. The situation is very complicated because the Christian Democratic party has little room to maneuver in its continuing efforts to find a formula for a stable coalition government. Although the extremist groups—Communist, Socialist, Fascist, Monarchist—have together usually obtained around a third of the Italian vote in parliamentary elections, they have been unacceptable to the Christian Democrats as partners in government. Consequently, the Christian Democrats have often had to base coalition governments on support from the small Social Democratic, Republican and Liberal parties. Such dependence has given them much greater bargaining power than their small numbers would have normally secured for them. The Social Democrats, and to a lesser extent the Republicans, have tried to push the coalition leftward, and the Liberals have pulled rightward. The Christian Democrats themselves have been pulled in various directions by their own internal disagreements. Since 1957 the government has often been composed only of Christian Democrats, and for survival in office has required the voting support or the benevolent abstention of other parties.

The Left wing of the Christian Democratic party has long believed in a coalition of Christian Democrats, Social Democrats, Republicans and Socialists as the only solution to the frequent changes of government. The Right wing has favored a coalition of Christian Democrats, Liberals and Monarchists. In 1958 Prime Minister Fanfani formed a leftward-oriented coalition of his own party and the Social Democrats in order to attract Socialist support and wean it away from the Communists. Conservative Christian Democrats strongly opposed the shift, the attempt was short-lived, and Fanfani resigned as secretary-general of the party. The Christian Democrats, therefore, turned in the other direction and set up a one-party Christian Democratic minority government under Antonio Segni, supported by their conservative elements. The growing leftward trend within the party continued to develop. In April 1960, another one-party Christian Democratic government under the late Fernando Tambroni was able to survive a confidence vote in the Chamber of Deputies only by accepting the votes of the Fascists. Too many Christian Democrats had fought in the Resistance in World War II to be willing to accept Fascist support. Several cabinet ministers, including the minister for southern development, the retired trade union leader, Giulio Pastore, resigned in protest. The Fascist votes were finally accepted only to allow the formation of a "caretaker" government which limped along for nearly two months.

By early 1962 it seemed that all the familiar possible permutations and combinations had been tried except for one alternative: the so-called Opening to the Left. By moving this way, the Christian Democrats believed they would not only follow the dictates of their own increasingly strong Left but would possibly bring the Socialists out of the wilderness of alliance with the Communists in which they had wandered thus far during the postwar period. The "opening," however, was not unopposed. Important conservative Christian Democrats, like former prime ministers Scelba and Pella, were against it, as were the Liberals. And of course for their own reasons, Communists,

Fascists and Monarchists also opposed it, as did the Left wing of the Socialist party.

Nonetheless, in February 1962, Premier Fanfani formed a new government made up of nineteen Christian Democrats, three Social Democrats and two Republicans. What made this coalition significant was that the Socialist party, as mentioned earlier, was pledged to support it "externally."...

Within the country the Opening to the Left received a mixed reception. It was supported by some leading industrialists such as seventy-nine-year-old Vittorio Valletta, president of Fiat [the giant automobile company], one of Italy's ablest and most enlightened employers, and by Count Carlo Faina, the forward-looking and astute president of Montecatini, Italy's largest chemical company. Other businessmen feared it heralded increasing nationalization and regulation of industry. Many people doubted that the Socialists had really loosened their ties with the Communists. Hopeful observers, on the other hand, believed that if the Socialists really had broken free, the opening would drain away working-class support from the Communists and ultimately leave them isolated. . . .

Since Italian political sentiment is still moving slightly leftward, the stage would appear to be set for the full-scale entry of the Socialists into the government. . . . The shifts in scene in Italy are perhaps too rapid to make such a prediction anything but premature. What will happen depends in large part on the ability of the parties involved to work together, on the effectiveness of the present government, on the shifting directions of currents within the parties themselves and on internal economic developments.

FORGETTING THE FASCIST INTERLUDE [2]

What do Italians born in the 1930's and 1940's know about Mussolini beyond the fact that he drained the Pontine Marshes? What do they know of his *squadristi* and castor-oil treatments and Pact of Steel with Hitler, of the Nazi occupation in Italy and the partisan Resistance?

[2] From "The Lost Decades in Italian History," by Claire Sterling, Mediterranean correspondent, *The Reporter*. *The Reporter*. 25:34-6. Jl. 6, '61. Copyright 1961 by The Reporter Magazine Company. Reprinted by permission.

The powerful obliterating force of time has been at work. There are, of course, some young men and women who feel strongly about fascism, one way or the other. But even these tend to see the era just preceding theirs through the lens of folklore, and an unnerving number of others seem as incurious and disengaged about it as they might be about the Boxer Rebellion.

Clearly, time alone cannot be blamed for this state of affairs: sixteen years aren't all that long. But time has been helped, in this case, by the disinclination of older Italians to talk about such painful memories, and still more by the fact that a whole generation has grown to manhood without learning a word on the subject in its schools.

It was . . . [not until 1960] that the government decided to permit the teaching of history from 1922—Year One of the Fascist Era—onward. Until then, all history had stopped, from primary school through the university, at the First World War; and many scholars felt that this was just as it should be. For a country shrouded in classic academic traditions, the idea of injecting shrill political controversy into the classroom was highly unorthodox. Moreover, to teach about fascism fully and fairly, with all its ignoble features—political oppression at home, predatory raids abroad, defeat and disgrace in war, fratricidal bloodshed—requires an exacting kind of patriotism as well as objectivity. No scholastic formulation, however guarded, could have failed to add one more scabrous issue to all the others in domestic politics; and no government since the Liberation had felt strong enough to face that. . . .

The . . . government of Amintore Fanfani . . . evidently decided that the immediate risk . . . [was] small compared to the risk of having a second generation reach voting age in political innocence.

> With the time that has elapsed and the objective evaluation that scholars have made [said the Minister of Education in his 1960 proclamation], these events [since 1922] have by now entered under the arch of history. They can no longer be ignored in official teaching, lest our youth should have an incomplete and insufficient knowledge of the new democratic order of the republic.

Admirable as the minister's intentions might have been, however, the results so far are discouraging. Actually, Italian scholars have done very little toward making an objective evaluation of Mussolini and his works. The fault is not entirely theirs, since all official documents on that period are locked up in the state archives, where probably they will stay for quite a while. . . .

Many textbooks suffer from a crippling reticence or deliberate deformation, or both. One of the most widely circulated high school history texts, for example, describes Mussolini's invasion of Ethiopia by saying: "Ethiopia came into conflict with Italy because of a violation of frontiers by the Ethiopians"; it adds that Mussolini attacked Greece because "Greece refused to join the tripartite Rome-Berlin-Tokyo alliance"; it goes on to explain that Mussolini sent his army to help Franco in Spain because, though Franco was rebelling against a legally elected government, that government was *"an anticlerical democratic republic* [author's italics] heading swiftly toward bolshevism, and imposed by a minority on a traditionally Catholic and monarchist nation"; and it clarifies Hitler's rise to power by saying: "In the uneasy period after the First World War, Germany suffered more than any other belligerent state; but, formed by a people with great moral resources and national pride, it did not take long to rise again." The same author devotes one line to anti-Semitism in Nazi Germany by referring to Hitler's "vexatious campaign against the Jews."

In another high school text, also widely circulated, most of Europe's troubles between the two world wars are ascribed to the Versailles Treaty, which, among other things, destroyed the Austro-Hungarian Empire, "that centuries-old bulwark of Latin-German civilization against the growing pressure of the Slavs"; the discontent caused by that treaty is described as having so disoriented Italian soldiers returning from the war that, "instigated by parties of the Left with a criminal propaganda of hatred against the ruling classes, they abandoned themselves to public demonstrations, and even fell so low as to occupy the factories"; and it was in this political debilitation, against which the "healthy part of the nation reacted," that Mussolini took on the task of rescuing the country from "the bolshevism spreading over the Peninsula." According to the same author, Mussolini was a man of "extraordinary dynamism . . . [and] an admirer of the history and grandeur of Rome . . . who let himself be seduced by the idea, noble in itself, of conferring similar fortunes on the New

Italy." It was with these "audacious aspirations," the author concludes, that "the Duce ruined himself and fascism." After his arrest on July 25, 1943, "The announcement of this extraordinary event immediately brought a wave of lively anti-Fascist agitation throughout Italy: the number of Fascist victims was very great."

These are egregious examples. But even in the less exuberant texts, the kind of facts that any citizen of a young and untried democracy like Italy's ought to know are often obscured or ignored altogether. In the high school and junior high texts particularly—and only a small fraction of Italy's youth goes on to college—the student is given to understand, by and large, that fascism arose in Italy as the only alternative to communism; that it was a more or less mild dictatorship (of the "rosewater" variety, as a university graduate in political science assured me); that the expansionist policies of Mussolini and Hitler both were simply a continuation of the pre-First World War struggle between have and have-not nations (with no indication that fascism might have had unusual historical characteristics); that the Second World War, therefore, was no different from the First (except that the second time Italy chose the losing side); that partisan fighters in the Resistance were on the same juridical, political, and moral plane as those who fought for Mussolini's puppet Salò Republic (formed by the Germans after the Duce had been overthrown); and that whatever might have gone wrong with Mussolini's plans, it was Britain, the United States, Haile Selassie, the League of Nations, Hitler, or at worst the Duce's sycophantic advisers who were to blame.

Rare are the textbooks that talk of Mussolini's responsibility for the murder of the Socialist leader Matteotti in 1924 (which marked the end of all liberty in Italy), or the Fascist *squadristi* who once roamed the country beating and killing opponents of the Duce, or the arrests, the torture, and the long prison sentences inflicted on Italian democrats. Even the massacre of more than three hundred Italian hostages in Rome's Ardeatine Caves—the primary symbol of Nazi brutality during Hitler's wartime occupation of Italy—is hardly ever mentioned.

It would be surprising, in these circumstances, if Italy's younger citizens could have a clear idea of the fears, hopes, suffering, and ideals that went into the founding of the present republic—all the more so since not many of them even have a clear idea of how the republic works. Until [1958] the schools here gave no instruction in civics. The function of the government and the rights and duties of its citizens were matters left to political parties or the press for explanation; and so little explaining was done that few Italians under thirty today could define precisely the powers of the president, or the division of powers among the state's executive, legislative, and judicial branches, or the other constitutional provisions.

Parliament tried to correct this in 1958 by ordering the addition of civics courses to the school syllabus at all levels. But with the syllabus running back to the founding of the Roman Empire, the average time devoted to this new subject has been about sixteen hours a year. Many teachers who know nothing about the material simply don't teach it; and here again, the textbooks are not excessively helpful. Of the fifty civics texts examined recently by the Committee for Cultural Freedom, directed by Ignazio Silone, only fifteen were found adequate. Among the others, one is apt to come across statements like "We have the fortune to live in a family and a state organized in an almost perfect manner, and we enjoy a splendid civilization," or "Woman has a fundamental and delicate function in society, in that every woman is or will be a mother." On occasion, the statements are a good deal more deadly. "Solely from the political point of view," says one widely used text, "the coming and continuance of the Fascist regime 'revolutionized' [author's quotes] the Italian state, transforming it from a liberal, democratic, and parliamentary state to an authoritarian and totalitarian one. But all this was done in the most orthodox legality. . . . A typical *coup d'état,* on the other hand, was the deposition of the Fascist regime on July 25, 1943, and thereafter." "No social organism can exist," says another popular text, "if the will of all men does not become a single will. No form of social life can be imagined without a guide, without those who command and those who obey. The social organism can survive and prosper, therefore, only when there exists within it a hierarchy among men, in the sense that some are given to lead and command, and all the others have the duty to let themselves be guided and obey."

While texts like these might give the impression that Italy's school system is riddled with Fascists, that isn't true. Many of the authors quoted here consider themselves democrats, and the teaching staffs have at least as many conscious anti-Fascists as Fascists. But the authors aren't all scholars, nor can they easily shake off the mental habits of a lifetime; and between the political extremes on the school faculties is a large body of overworked and underpaid teachers whose chief concern is to stay out of trouble, and who have no particular views on anything at all. For them, the republic, the constitution, and the Resistance seem somehow to be delicate and vaguely dangerous themes; and they feel it is unpleasant and unsafe, as well as unpatriotic, to dwell on the disagreeable aspects of their country's recent past. In this regard, there isn't much doubt that they reflect a considerable body of public opinion.

Italy has been a unified state for only a hundred years and a democratic republic for only fifteen, with twenty-two years of fascism in between. The Italians haven't had much time, therefore, to accumulate lasting democratic traditions in politics. Unless the gaps in their educational system are repaired, three generations of them will have had no chance to pick up the elementary principles of democratic thinking in the schools.

The fact that most Italians have stuck to democracy since the republic was formed is a tribute to their moral quality. For the most part, these are people who have lived through fascism, and therefore know what democracy *isn't.* The time is coming soon when the overwhelming majority of voters will not even have had such experience to go by. Whether or not these younger Italians are alone in their prevailing attitudes of indifference and noncommitment—and these seem to be a universal mark of our times—a disturbing number are nevertheless indifferent and uncommitted. Under these conditions, one can't help wondering how long the republic can continue to resist the encroaching totalitarian movements of both Right and Left by relying on the instincts rather than on the training of its citizens.

THE 1963 ELECTIONS [3]

The . . . elections [of 1963] can hardly be said to have settled Italy's political problems. The new Parliament is just a little worse than the last two, which were nearly unworkable. The

[3] From "The Italian Elections: Even Worse than Before," by Claire Sterling, Mediterranean correspondent, *The Reporter*. *The Reporter*. 28:22-5. My. 23, '63. Copyright 1963 by The Reporter Magazine Company. Reprinted by permission.

Communists will be stronger this time, their share of the vote having gone up from 22 per cent to 25 per cent, whereas the ruling Christian Democrats have dropped from 42 per cent to 38 per cent, losing all but a theoretical freedom of choice. Like the outgoing parliament, the new one offers them no practical alternative to a coalition with the Socialists—which they accepted in principle when Premier Amintore Fanfani's Center-Left cabinet was formed. But they will be going into negotiations now as the only heavy losers in these elections, enabling the Socialists, who lost only 0.4 per cent, to set the terms. A shotgun wedding of this kind is not likely to bring five years of domestic peace.

Apart from an alliance with the Socialists, the Christian Democrats have only two mathematical possibilities of forming a majority coalition now. One would be with the Liberals and Fascists. But even if the Catholic party would risk a partnership with the Fascists after its calamitous experiment in that direction in 1960, the conservative but democratic Liberal party has already said it would not. The other would be a Center coalition with the Liberals and Social Democrats, which the Social Democrats have long since rejected in principle and have every reason now to reject in practice: their support of the Center-Left formula has brought them 528,000 new votes in this election, raising their share of the total from 4.4 to 6.3 per cent and greatly increasing their influence. The Liberals' gain, most of it drawn from the moribund Monarchist party, was even greater, from 3.5 to 7 per cent. They have become the fourth ranking Italian party.

It will be some time before the Christian Democrats can take a calm, reflective view of the new situation, not only in terms of their party but of the whole Center-Left experiment. The experiment had been conceived as the only way to stem the Communist tide and to modernize the country socially, juridically, fiscally, and educationally, so as to meet the needs of a rapidly expanding economy. The undertaking could not be expected to get results in barely a year. The two biggest parties concerned, in fact, had both anticipated a setback in these elections, with some conservative Christian Democrats switching to the free-enterprise Liberal party and a comparable number of Socialists going over to the Communists. Then, with the elections out of the way and the balance of power presumably unchanged, the Center-Left parties could get down to business, hoping to be rewarded for their efforts in the next elections, five years hence.

Things have not turned out quite that way. True, the combined vote of all the Center-Left parties—Christian Democratic, Social Democratic, Republican, Socialist—came to 58 per cent, indicating that well over half the electorate either approves of the experiment or doesn't disapprove violently enough to bolt party lines in protest. Nevertheless, the balance of power within the coalition has shifted appreciably; the Christian Democrats' vote has been whittled away, with practically all the whittling done by their Social Democratic and Socialist partners, and a great number of voters did not stop there but went straight on to the Communist party. With more than a million votes added to the 6.7 million they had before, the Communists can rightfully claim to be the real winners—and they do.

Two elements in these elections may help to explain what happened. For one thing, the Socialists were in the government orbit for the first time since the war, a fact that was bound to alter the traditional voting habits of the Italian working class. The change left no choice of parties for the workers who wanted to express a protest for all sorts of reasons: because they hadn't gotten enough out of the economic boom, or had gotten enough to want more, or resented some social injustice, or simply assumed—as many other Italians do—that any government, whatever its pretensions, must be a den of thieves. The Communists, therefore, were left alone to catch an always sizable if sometimes frivolous antigovernment vote, and by "reaping their neighbor's field," as the Communist leader Palmiro Togliatti advised, they also picked up the votes of many Socialists who, clinging to their old faith in working-class unity, strongly disapproved of their party's desertion to the capitalist camp.

At least as important an element was the shift in the Catholic Church. From the time he was elected in 1958, Pope John XXIII . . . [showed] an increasing desire to break through the barriers that have sealed the Church off from a Communist world that now contains a third of the human race. He . . . made a continuing effort to establish the conditions for a *modus vivendi* with communism, especially within the past year. The pointed failure of the Ecumenical Council to speak out against communism, the spectacular visit of Khrushchev's son-in-law to the Pope in the middle of the election campaign, and, also in the middle of the campaign, the *Pacem in Terris* encyclical which removed much of the stigma that the Church had placed on communism in the past—all have helped to lower the Catholics' once rigid anti-Communist guard, and the Italian Communist party has made the most of the situation.

This result has certainly shocked the Church hierarchy, which, in moving along the new course, had obviously been thinking in terms of a billion people rather than of the 50 million in Italy. Though the Christian Democrats too had sought to exploit the encyclical, they were plainly the losers by it. Italy's ruling party had come into being primarily to provide a democratic vehicle for all the disparate Catholic voters whose greatest concern was to stop communism. It has acquired other important functions, and indeed has adopted much more advanced economic and social policies than anyone would have expected a few years back. But where anticommunism has been the Christian Democrats' strongest unifying force, their social and economic policies have been perpetually divisive. With the emphasis shifting from the one to the other, many Catholic voters felt free to pick another party in these elections.

Whatever the other reasons for the Communist advance and the Christian Democratic decline, both of these elements will have a serious effect on the incoming Center-Left government. There doesn't seem to be much chance now that the Catholics and Socialists will work together with the give-and-take that the experiment needs. Each side, in fact, is liable to become a good deal tougher. . . .

Given the disarray caused by the maneuverings of the recent past, Italy badly needed a government with clear and clearly agreed-upon policies that could count on a stable majority in Parliament. But the recent elections have made the emergence of such effective leadership more unlikely than ever.

UNDERSTANDING ITALY'S VOTE [4]

How did the Communists manage to poll a million votes more [in the elections of April 1963] than they did in the previous

[4] From article by Mauro Calamandrei, Italian newspaper correspondent. *New Leader*. 46:14-15. My. 27, '63. Reprinted by permission.

general election, in 1958, while Pietro Nenni's Left-wing Socialists held their own and the Social Democrats improved their position considerably? Where did the Liberals, who better than doubled their 1958 total, pick up their new strength? If the electorate this year was more disposed to progressive measures than in the past, why did it repudiate the first Christian Democratic government that sought to institute such measures? And why, if the voters were rejecting the idea of continuing the Opening to the Left, did they give greater support to the Left than to the Right?

The Communist vote is worth considering first because it reflects many features common to the entire Italian situation. The Communists picked up most of their increase from new voters, from the Left wing of the Nenni Socialists and, to a lesser extent, from former Monarchists, neo-Fascists and Christian Democrats. And the reason for this is to be found in the great social transformation that has occurred in Italy during the past five years.

Hundreds of thousands of Italians have left their small villages in the south for the northern industrial centers of Turin and Milan; or have emigrated to Switzerland, France or Germany; or simply have moved to the new industrial districts in Naples, Taranto and other southern cities. In 1958, these people voted the way their parish priest or town landowner asked them to vote. Many were so indifferent to politics that they exchanged their ballot for a pair of shoes, a letter of introduction or even a dish of spaghetti. Not too long ago Achille Lauro, the Monarchist mayor of Naples, distributed one shoe to his "clients" before election, the second shoe afterward; the faithful were also rewarded with great spaghetti parties.

Once starving farm workers join a gang of miners or enter an industrial plant, however, they quickly acquire the democratic spirit. Their erstwhile fatalism is transformed into anger over past and present injustices, often making them advocates of radical political positions.

Today the political education of the migrant reaches back into the villages. When at Christmas or Easter, at vacation or election time, the young people return home with new suits and transistor radios, they also bring to their families new ideas and habits. The youth who have remained at home, even the women, are more inclined to listen to them than to the old father or grandfather.

Thus, in many peasant families the Right-wing vote of yesterday has become the Communist vote of today.

But the Communists have gained votes not only in south and among the new urban immigrants; they have also increased their strength among the native workers in Turin and in the small towns of Tuscany and Emilia. Full employment has given the labor unions the power to bargain hard for a greater share of the national income. . . . Thousands of those who belong to Christian Democratic and Social Democratic unions apparently voted the Communist list as a protest to the government against the slow realization of the social goals of the Opening to the Left.

In certain communities of the north and center of Italy, though, the Communist gains also stemmed from opposition to the growing cooperation between Christian Democrats and Socialists. These are communities with a long leftist tradition, but while the voters sympathize with the formation of a progressive national government, they fear the application of the same formula on the local level. In many such towns an alliance of Communists and Socialists—which in some cases includes members of other secular leftist groups—has ruled since the end of the war. Rome has repeatedly used its control over these local municipalities as a political weapon, with the result that many Communist or front administrations have become the most efficient and honest in the country. The local people are proud of their leaders and have no wish to change.

Frequently, too, the threat to the status quo in these communities is not limited to public affairs. At stake as well are local interests in cooperatives and stores, kindergartens and schools, recreation centers and adult education institutes, and hundreds of small companies created by workers who now share in their ownership. In past years, a large part of the Communist vote was made up of indigent farmers, angry and/or poor intellectuals and frustrated minorities. This hard core still exists, but with the coming of the new prosperity the party now has the allegiance of many small-time industrialists and master builders, shop-owners and merchants who associate their economic well-being and social status with the Communists and vote Communist as a guarantee of conservatism. Similarly, there are some Nenni Socialists who vote Communist to preserve the status quo in their communities.

In some areas, therefore, the Italian Communist party is as firmly entrenched as the Republican party was for so long in Vermont or the Dakotas. It is a party of the local ruling groups, largely managerial in function and fairly indifferent and independent of the central party headquarters in Rome. Even national prosperity has helped the Communist cause. Many people openly admit they would not have voted for the Communists if there had been any chance of the party winning a majority.

Last but hardly least, the Communist electoral success is due to the astuteness of Palmiro Togliatti, the party's long-time leader. Togliatti has made the party a home and a refuge for a wide range of different types: the intellectual with vague populist leanings, the poor farm worker who admires the revolutionary spirit of the Chinese Communists, the skilled worker with expectations that rise faster than his salary, the craftsman who has grown fat and conservative over the years.

In contrast, now that the international situation no longer permits the party in power to put national unity above all other issues, the Christian Democrats have certainly suffered from trying to be too many things to too many people. Right-wing commentators have blamed the loss in CD strength on several factors: the fear of radical changes among many voters; the Church's failure to exert moral pressure on the electorate, as it has in the past; the promulgation of the papal encyclical *Peace on Earth;* and even the meeting . . . between . . . Pope [John XXIII] and Alexei Adzhubei, Khrushchev's personal emissary. But while it is apparent that hundreds of thousands who once considered the Catholic party a fortress of conservatism voted for the Liberals (actually, despite the name, a conservative group), it is doubtful whether any of the other factors cited had much to do with the election's outcome.

True, some of the CD's electoral losses are due to the Opening to the Left. What the critics of the Right fail to mention, however, is that these losses might have been much greater had the party decided on a Right-leaning coalition. The electoral success not only of the Communists but also of the Nenni Socialists and the Social Democrats indicates that many Italians want the government to commit itself more seriously to a progressive program. The Socialists are organizationally weak and the poorest of the Italian political parties; they could not have withstood the violent

Communist attacks without genuine mass support. The gains of the Social Democrats are even more significant; their leader, Giuseppe Saragut, has consistently supported the Opening to the Left, without any weakening of the Western Alliance. The party's improved position is open endorsement of this policy.

On the whole, in fact, Italians this year showed more interest and discrimination in concrete political issues than at any time since 1948, when the Christian Democrats took over the reins of government. Considering the natural erosion of public confidence in any group that has ruled continuously for fifteen years, and the additional damage done to the CD by recent revelations of corruption among highly placed political figures, it is remarkable that the Christian Democrats did not incur greater losses.

In the end, then, the election may be a healthy sign for Italian democracy. Even the fact that the . . . Left-Center coalition can no longer rule without the open support of the Nenni Socialists may prove a blessing in disguise. It confronts both the Socialists and the Christian Democrats with an opportunity, if not the necessity, of realistically facing the problems of governmental responsibility.

YOUNG COMMUNISTS [5]

The Communist party's success at the . . . [1963] Italian elections represents an indication of the dissatisfaction of the younger generations with the prevailing order of things.

It is also a reminder that, to a considerable extent, a skillful presentation of ideas as well as material progress moves and motivates those born after World War II, when an acceleration of history of unparalleled dimensions ushered in one of the most profound revolutions of all time.

Thus, unless there are profound changes, the Communists' progress may well win new advances in the future.

There seems to be little doubt but that Italy's youth gave Palmiro Togliatti's party its biggest boost in years.

The strength of the other leftist groupings remained stationary or emerged slightly improved. That would hint that the Communists did not gain at the expense of the other parties of the

[5] From "Youths Boost Italian Reds," by Mario Rossi, Italian newspaper correspondent. *The Christian Science Monitor* (Eastern edition). p 11. My. 2, '63. Reprinted by permission.

Left. It can be reasonably assumed also that they did not gain at the expense of the parties of the Center and the Right.

The only conclusion can be that there was an inflow of new votes, that the new generation voting for the first time supported in large numbers the Communist party.

Economic conditions help explain this trend up to a point.

Italy's economic boom of the last few years has spread only partially to the economically lower classes. They not only remain poor, but resentful of the new wealth acquired by the middle and upper classes.

The realization of the persistence of poverty often acquires deep social implications that carry over into the political field.

Years ago, this reporter visited a village in southern Italy which had been hardly reached by civilization and where life went on more or less as it had for centuries. A majority of the population, among the poorest in Europe, voted for the Christian Democrats, the Fascists, and the Monarchists.

When he revisited the village a year later, it had undergone a deep change. The government had introduced land reform and spent millions of lire in new housing projects and to bring water and electricity into the village.

Strange as it may seem, that same village also began giving a substantial number of votes to the Communist party.

When this reporter asked why, he was told that, for the government, reform was a matter of political expediency while, for the Communists, it was a matter of principle. By voting Communist they thought they would make sure that what was given them would not be taken away.

Socially, Italy has not moved ahead with the times, but at the same time it has shown that progress is possible and that poverty need not be the unchangeable lot of the masses.

The Communists offer a program of social change that millions of people obviously consider convincing, well planned, and reasonably moderate. They have succeeded in making it largely acceptable because they themselves have become socially acceptable.

Representing a fourth of the adult population, the Communist could not possibly be represented as the dangerous terrorist out to subvert what most Italians consider dear. He is the butcher around the corner, the professor of the university, the journalist with whom you have interminable debates at some Roman *trattoria* (restaurant); quite often your cousin, or brother, or closest friend with whom you went through school.

This acceptability has been augmented—it would be self-defeating to ignore it—by the immense competence of the Italian Communist party's boss, Palmiro Togliatti, one of the most astute politicians in the world, and a very cultivated man.

It must also be remembered that whatever smacks of fascism produces revulsion, especially in the younger generations. The execution in Spain a few days prior to the Italian elections of the Communist leader, Julian Grimau, caused an almost physical sense of disgust in a large segment of the population. In other words, the Franco regime gave the Italian Communists large numbers of votes.

In a larger sense, the progress of the Left, Communist and non-Communist, expresses a search for new ways, a longing for a better society.

ITALY'S LEFTIST INTELLECTUALS [6]

"Everyone knows that the only worth-while people in Italy today are leftists."

This remark, dropped casually by a hostess at a Roman dinner party not long ago, brought not a flicker of disagreement from the guests. It is generally accepted by Italians now that many of their leading intellectuals—particularly those of international stature—are either pro-Communist or very far to the non-Communist Left.

Until recently this political inclination of the intellectuals was dismissed as being exotic and comparatively harmless; but the increase of one million Communist votes and the corresponding decrease in Christian Democratic votes in the . . . [1963] elections have lent new weight to their position. To the intellectuals, in turn, the voting represents a kind of victory. First, it comes at a time of unprecedented prosperity (most experts predicted a drop in Communist strength), so the Communist gain cannot be explained away as the usual protest by discontented or unemployed workers; second, the increase comes when the Italian Communist

[6] From "Italy's Intellectuals Steer to the Left," by Joan Marble Cook, American journalist living in Rome. New York *Times Magazine*. p 32+. My. 26, '63. Copyright by The New York Times. Reprinted by permission.

party has been losing members, and thus it cannot be argued that the million new Communist supporters are merely card-carrying hacks.

The appearance of the new Communist voter is particularly gratifying to Left-wing intellectuals because he seems to be corroborating the mood of protest that dominates the intellectuals themselves. Considering that this mood has now received such impressive popular support, it is especially worth while to examine the intellectual's attitude and to try to explain what kind of man he is and why he thinks as he does.

Who are Italy's Left-wing intellectuals?

They are important people—leaders in the world of art, literature and the theater—the cultural celebrities of Italy. Consider the membership of the "Solidarity with Castro Committee," formed at the time of the Cuban crisis, whose adherents marched the streets of Rome to protest "American imperialism." The list read like a "Who's Who" of Italian culture; it included Alberto Moravia, the best-selling novelist; Carlo Levi, the painter and author of *Christ Stopped at Eboli;* Luchino Visconti, director of *Rocco and His Brothers* and *The Leopard;* Cesare Zavattini, the film writer and author of *Miracle in Milan;* Valerio Zurlini, director of *The Girl with the Suitcase;* Michelangelo Antonioni, the director of *L'Avventura;* Renato Guttuso, the painter; Pier Paolo Pasolini, director of *Mama Roma.*

After Premier Khrushchev had finally packed up his missiles and taken them out of Cuba, his Italian supporters inked up their mimeograph machines and let go with a new manifesto calling for the speedy removal of all American missile bases from Italian soil. In addition to the pro-Castro group, the backers of this new manifesto included Salvatore Quasimodo, the Nobel prize poet; Mario Soldati, the novelist; Elio Vittorini, the author of *The Light and the Dark*; and such artists as Giacomo Manzu, Vespignani and Maffei.

Foreign observers noted that only a few names in the entire hierarchy of Italian culture seemed to be missing—not listed were novelist Ignazio Silone (one of the few outspoken anti-Communist intellectuals in Italy); Federico Fellini, the film director, a perennial nonjoiner; and director and actor Vittorio de Sica, who has often supported Left-wing causes and was possibly out of town when the manifesto was signed.

The Communist party naturally made the most of these manifestoes; party leader Palmiro Togliatti, who has been hard put to stir up even a small street demonstration in recent years, went around congratulating himself on the intellectuals' militant stand.

Actually, Togliatti was taking more credit than he deserved; the Italian intellectuals are not all obedient to his command. Their attitude toward him and toward the party varies from general subservience to broad suspicion.

The more one studies their behavior, the more one becomes convinced that their demonstrations are not so much for Togliatti or against America; they are staged primarily for the benefit of other Italians. The intellectuals' protests are essentially protests against a general Italian condition; they seem to want to show by their demonstrations that there are still people in Italy who care about *something*.

In this they give utterance to a widespread mood. It is difficult to exaggerate the feeling of malaise that has been gripping Italy during the past year. Everywhere one goes, one finds a kind of revulsion against laxity in public and private standards. . . .

"Nobody hates politicians as much as the Italians," says a leading Milanese magazine. This is quite true. Ask any Italian, whether he is a Liberal, Fascist, Christian Democrat or Communist, what he thinks of politicians and a look of outrage and revulsion will come over his face.

To the intellectuals, who are far more sensitive than the average voter, the feeling of malaise is almost insupportable. It obsesses them. Moravia writes one book after another about the decay and corruption of the middle classes. Fellini, Visconti and Antonioni examine the evils of Italian society with the fascination of scientists studying a virus.

> Italy is a very sick country [explained film writer Zavattini not long ago]. It is a country of adulterers. It is a country of tax dodgers. It is a country that has never had a real democracy. The small cures and compromises won't work any longer. What we need is a radical change of the government and of the people. If the situation isn't urgent now, when will it ever be?

The despair and indignation of the intellectuals is understandable, but the question remains. Why have nearly all of them gone Left?

Italian history provides the answer. They have gone Left because they believe there is no alternative. The Center means the same old muddle. The Right, to Italian intellectuals, means fascism or the Church. Both choices are unthinkable; France may have its respected Catholic intellectuals but Italy has none. To be an intellectual in Italy means to be in revolt, to be ready to throw out the old, discredited ruling class and make a clean break with the past.

The fact that this position accidentally helps Russia and hurts the United States gives the intellectuals no sleepless nights. In fact, they may even get a certain satisfaction from it.

It is hard to know whether the intellectuals have faced up to the consequences of their actions. Do they really hope and expect that their campaign will bring communism to Italy? It seems doubtful. Are they really so anti-American that they are prepared to turn their backs completely on all their traditional friends in Europe and across the Atlantic? No one knows. One can only guess.

Certainly when they discuss America and Russia, they have a tendency to emphasize the faults of America, quoting at great length from United States films, novels and popular sociology books, while finding excuses for Russia. Again and again they talk about the way "things are going to be" in Russia. When they talk about America, they are more specific and speak of McCarthy and the McCarran Act.

Their first complaint against the United States is invariably a political one. Carlo Levi, a newly elected Communist senator and one of the foremost apologists for Russia, presents their position in this way:

> Back in the thirties and forties the United States seemed to be a paradise to Italian intellectuals. We read Hemingway, Faulkner, Steinbeck and Dos Passos and they had an enormous influence upon us. I wrote an article right after the war called "The Myth of America" in which I tried to show how America had become the hope of European liberals.
>
> Our first disappointment came with the American military government which lost no time in supporting all the most backward and moribund elements in Italy. We were further disillusioned when we found the United States propping up other tired and reactionary governments around the world.

To the intellectuals, any nation that willingly places itself in this position is either "*sciocco*" (stupid) or acting out of the most dangerous kind of self-interest.

Their second argument is that the old bogyman "American materialism," with its automobiles and transistor radios, is ruining gracious old Italy. (To this charge one might reply that materialism has been a way of life in Italy since Columbus set off across the Atlantic.) The intellectuals follow this argument with a series of clichés about "alienation," "conformity" and the "separation of man from his roots." If pressed, however, they will admit that perhaps conformity is not so much an American product as it is a product of the machine age. One suspects that the alienation that really upsets them is their own alienation from their fellow Italians.

The picture changes when the talk shifts to Russia. A handful of the intellectuals are actual party members. Others admire Russia and the Russians; still others are skeptical. Levi, for instance, claims that he finds in Russia "a basic attachment to human values and to the old European verities" that he finds nowhere else. Moravia is at best a lukewarm Russophile.

"There is no liberty for the individual in Russia," Moravia said in an interview. "Many of us in Italy are attracted to the ideas of Marxism, but we do not think those ideas have been carried out in Russia."

Moravia's idea is echoed, with variations, by other members of the intellectual group. They believe that if communism ever came to Italy, it would be a milder form. Communism today seems to have lost some of its bite. Togliatti never talks about a revolution. The horrors of Hungary are past. Khrushchev seems to be mellowing and his son-in-law was cordially received by . . . Pope [John XXIII].

To many intellectuals, Russia is a fine place to visit (it pays special royalties to admiring foreign authors) although they wouldn't want to live there. They, too, admire the "human values" of the Russians, but they would probably stop short of swapping them for their well-cut British suits and their General Electric refrigerators. The mind reels to think of the aristocratic film director, Luchino Visconti, giving up his summer villa on Ischia and his luxurious home in Rome to move to Moscow. Nor can one think of individualists like Zavattini willingly harnessing their talents to the service of the Russian state or meekly accepting cultural dictation from above.

The recent Soviet dictum against abstract art embarrassed the Italian intellectuals and it took them a while before they could prod Carlo Levi into making a semiofficial response. Said Levi about the art rumpus:

> As a painter and a man of liberty, I do not like it. But still, even if those Russian abstract painters are not allowed to exhibit, they can go on painting. I was not allowed to exhibit from 1933 until 1947 by the Fascists in Italy, but I painted anyhow and I did the best work of my career. I think that those Russian painters can resist that kind of state pressure because it is exterior. It does not destroy their inner liberty. There is another kind of pressure that exists in the United States and Italy and France that corrupts much more—the pressure to paint a certain way because it sells and is fashionable. This kind of corruption is, I think, far worse than what is happening in Russia.

This kind of reasoning is not untypical of the Italian intellectuals. One suspects that they are waving banners that look bright in the sunlight without really understanding what the banners mean. The danger, of course, is that the intellectuals' arguments may attract discontented people, and there is a great deal of discontent in Italy today.

Some people, especially the young and impressionable, may listen to famous writers like Levi and say—why not? As the literacy rate grows, more and more educated and sensitive Italians may decide that the intellectuals have found the right answers and they may turn Left. Should this trend ever happen to coincide with a depression, the new unaffiliated Communist sympathizers might join with discontented and unemployed workers to sweep the Communists into power.

Another big danger is that there are almost no anti-Communist intellectuals of the first rank who are willing to roll up their sleeves and fight. Some journalists try, but it is hard for journalists to be taken seriously in Italy because so many of them are on political payrolls.

The man who is generally expected to lead the fight is Ignazio Silone. He was one of the organizers of the Communist party in Italy in the twenties and presumably knows what real communism is all about. Silone, however, takes the view that the

Left-wingers are superficial and self-seeking and that there is no point in paying too much attention to them.

> Many of these people are without profound political beliefs [Silone said], and they joined the Left wing out of snobbism. They have never demonstrated very strong character and they are likely to change their views at a moment's notice. There is a cultural industry here in Italy which makes personalities out of some of the intellectuals and they enjoy the limelight. . . .

However one evaluates their position, the intellectuals cannot be dismissed out of hand, because their ranks include some of the finest minds in Italy. They may be snobs, but they are also the people who worry about individual freedom. They may be opportunists, but they are concerned about corruption in the government and interference by the Church. They may be publicity hounds, but they try, as no other Italians do, to show in their books and films what is wrong with Italy and what needs to be corrected.

They consider themselves the keepers of the Italian conscience and they appear to be the kind of concerned citizens to whom American ideals would appeal. They loved America in the thirties; their art is much closer to American art than it is to Soviet art. Their books sell well in the United States. Yet despite all these things, they are drawn toward communism. The fact that America no longer kindles their imaginations is one of the ironies of our time.

CATHOLIC—YET COMMUNIST—WHY? [7]

Italian Communists have been making threats and demands not heard in Italy for more than a decade. Palmiro Togliatti, often rated the ablest and cleverest of Communist leaders this side of the Soviet Union, not only has demanded entry of the Communists into any future government, but has threatened trouble if Communist wishes are again ignored. There is a touch of impudence in these menacing suggestions, but they also reflect new strength, new confidence, one can even say new stature, for the Communist party in Italy.

[7] From article by Robert Neville, free-lance writer living in Italy. New York *Times Magazine*. p 12+. Je. 2, '63. Copyright by The New York Times. Reprinted by permission.

Behind Togliatti's boldness is . . . [the 1963] election in which the Communists captured more than a million new votes over those of the last general election in 1958. Some 7.7 million Italian voters out of a total of 31 million voted Communist.

The increased Communist showing, followed by the party's demands, has brought on a rash of political post-mortems. Togliatti himself said the vote was due to the "big zone of discontent and of real irritation that now exists in Italy." Not only have professional politicians, high and low, on municipal, provincial and national levels, pondered deeply the results of the recent balloting, but journalists, priests, industrialists, union leaders and just plain citizens have also joined in a sort of national soul-searching.

Why, oh why, it has been asked time and again, in an Italy with a Catholic population of 99 per cent plus, does one out of every four voters cast his ballot for a party which, even though it may now soft-pedal the issue, is basically against all religion? How can a considerable segment of a nation which accepts the Roman Pontiffs as Vicars of Jesus Christ, which looks up to them as fatherly and benevolent overseers of their affairs and which cheers them by the hundreds of thousands whenever they appear —how can such people turn around and vote for a party which, if it came to power, would certainly do its best to destroy the influence and prestige of the Papacy?

Some Italian newspapers, quite a few political commentators and numerous individual voters have blamed the increase on the Vatican itself. *Il Tempo* of Rome for example, cited the recent series of Vatican-Russian exchanges as being responsible for "disarming" many Italian voters into an acceptance of Communist candidates. These exchanges include the visit of Vatican representatives to Moscow and the subsequent invitation of Russian Orthodox prelates to the Ecumenical Council; the extended negotiations for the release of incarcerated Catholic bishops in Eastern Europe; the audience granted . . . by Pope John XXIII to Alexei Adzhubei, son-in-law of Premier Khrushchev and by his own boasting a "convinced atheist"; and finally the publication . . . of the encyclical, *Pacem in Terris*, generally regarded as a papal endorsement of "practical cooperation" between Christians and Marxists. . . .

Some Vatican officials will concede—rather reluctantly—that certain aspects of the new let's-talk-it-over-with-the-Communists policy might have been better timed. But, granting purely for the sake of argument that Vatican policy might have had something to do with the 3 per cent more of Italian voters who this year increased the Communist vote to a whopping 25 per cent of the total, there still remains the question of why 22 per cent have voted Communist in every election since the last war.

The basic fact is that Italians long ago acquired the habit of accepting the Church's ministrations for baptisms, marriages and deaths but of ignoring the Church's advice when entering the ballot booth. This was so even long before the emblem of the hammer and sickle began appearing.

Catholicism is the established state religion of Italy, but in the average Italian voter's mind Church and state have long been separate. The distinction between what is Caesar's and what is God's is deeply ingrained. The Italian nation itself was born in a moment of violent anticlericalism. Italian nationalism was an act of defiance of priests, bishops and popes. The residue of this anticlericalism has always made the Church's attempts to influence elections a very risky business.

Besides the religious question, others dealing with economic factors have been very much in order these past few weeks. This "clamorous success" for communism . . . comes after five years of an industrial boom during which stupendous yearly increases in national income have been registered. The Italian "economic miracle" has been fervently admired not only in Europe but also in America. Unemployment, which only a few years back seemed endemic, is being rapidly eliminated. In many parts of the country there is now an actual shortage of labor. Most of the indices of an unprecedented prosperity induced by a rapidly expanding capitalist economy are evident throughout the peninsula: cities and highways jammed with new cars, television forests covering every rooftop, new housing stretching endlessly in virtually every suburb of every city. And still, not only do the Communists not lose votes but they pick up more than a million in the bargain.

Notwithstanding the miracle, Togliatti is doubtless right when he talks about a "big zone of discontent." Affluence can create problems just as poverty can. The Communists have benefited by a protest vote which keeps accumulating year by year, election by election. Conditions have indeed improved, but they could have improved much more. Progress has been made but there could have been more progress. The miracle, alas, has not benefited everybody. The protest probably represents irritation more than deep-rooted dissatisfaction but it expresses itself at the polls just the same.

Italy is in a phase of fantastically rapid transition. Hundreds of thousands of Italians have been uprooted, lifted almost bodily out of the routine of a simple agricultural society and pitchforked into strange, highly organized complex industrial surroundings.

Almost two million workers from the south have migrated northward during the past five years in search of work. This upheaval has created its own problems and discomforts—terrible housing shortages, inadequate transportation, faulty utilities, an almost pathetic lack of schools, nurseries and playgrounds—all this plus an intense nostalgia.

In most northern cities the southerners have been segregated in unspeakable slums. At the same time the cost of living has risen sharply (10 per cent in the last year)—mostly, of course because of higher wages demanded by the very workers who now complain of the rising costs.

Alone of the traditional parties, the Communists seemed to have grasped that in this vast human displacement lay an opportunity to make friends and influence voters. The other parties continued to deal in programs and platforms, but the Communists thought in terms of practical help. Just as Tammany Hall workers once used to meet the immigrant ships arriving in New York harbor, so local Communist committees in the major northern cities were assigned to meet the immigrant trains arriving from the south.

These party workers took the southerners literally in hand, showed them how to look for work, taught them where to find living quarters, made them feel at home in the local Communist headquarters, which soon became virtually their clubhouses. The Communists organized sports events, ran day nurseries for working mothers, became adept even at holding beauty contests for the election of various local "Misses."

The testimony of Luigi Spataro, originally from a small village in Lucania, now an electrical factory worker in Genoa, is perhaps typical.

> The Communists were the only ones who seemed to care what happened to us when we moved north [Spataro says]. They showed me how to look for my first job. They taught me how to stand up for my rights. They showed me where we could find living quarters. Of course, I joined the Communist union. And of course, I voted the Communist ticket.

A highly educated woman social worker in Turin, a city flooded by wave after wave of southern immigrants these past few years, maintained that private philanthropy could do only a tiny fraction of what should be done.

> Only the Communists have realized the need for organized social work on a big scale to get these immigrants adjusted in their new homes. It's no wonder the immigrants turn around and vote Communist.

In Genoa, where southern migration has been particularly heavy, the Communist party is now the leading political organization. In Turin and Milan the Communists now run neck and neck for first place with the Christian Democrats, who once had absolute majorities, again thanks to the new immigrant vote. In the central Italian regions such as Tuscany, Umbria and Emilia, the Red vote has leaped far ahead, from roughly 30 per cent in most places to just under 40 per cent. Florence Communist headquarters can now boast that the party took more than 50 per cent of the vote in more than half the towns of the province. The Communist press now refers to the strip of central Italy from the Gulf of Genoa across the Adriatic as the "Red belt."

The Communists in Italy have learned, as has no other party, the fine political art of being all things to all men at all times. In Emilia they champion the rights of farm hands. In the Veneto they raise the standard of the dirt farmer with private holdings. In some places the party stands up for small shopworkers while in other places it claims to be the party of industrial workers. The Red mayor of Poggibonsi, a town of some 20,000 in Siena Province, generally rated the Reddest in all Italy, makes the extraordinary claim that of 230 store-owners in his community 120 are registered members of the Communist party.

The protest vote arises from a multitude of complaints. One voter in Milan says he voted Red because his monthly rent was raised from $40 to $45. "The government should not allow this to happen," he says. A housewife in Rome says she turned to the Communists when the bus service in her neighborhood became intolerable. A retired civil servant in Florence complained that he could no longer make do on his pension and therefore turned to the Communists. A worker in Bari said: "We workers have to pay taxes while the rich manage to avoid them." The Communists appear to be the beneficiaries of whatever complaint the citizenry has against the government.

La Stampa of Turin, one of Italy's outstanding journals, received a total of 587 letters from new voters on the theme "Why I Voted Communist." The letters covered a variety of subjects from high rents to the cost of onions, from the scandals that have occurred in high places to the fact that the government has spent too much money on helping the south, from dislike of the local parish priest to the inadequacies of public services.

But what struck the editors of *La Stampa* was that not one single letter writer said he voted Communist because he believed in communism, not one complained of the bad features of capitalism or mentioned such matters as the nationalization of property.

Not one talked of the glorious Soviet Union or the ignominious United States of America. In fact, not one brought up international affairs or Communist theory. Everybody without exception had voted for Communist candidates, it seems, only because he wanted to protest against the government.

Many Italians will insist that the one-in-four Communist vote is nothing to worry about. "You Americans have fixations," says Giuseppe Saragat, the Right-wing Socialist leader. At Christian Democratic party headquarters one leader echoed the same sentiment: "You Americans are given to overdramatization. Don't be so alarmed. The Communists are not about to take over Italy. We Christian Democrats are still far and away the largest party in the country."

More than one Italian polled on the subject suggested that his people are past masters at the art of political brinkmanship.

They vote for Communist candidates merely to scare the government in power into doing better.

One of *La Stampa's* letter writers confessed: "I cast my vote this time to put the fear of God into the powers that be. It's my only way of protesting." A young woman clerk in a Milan department store admitted, "I voted Communist in order to admonish and alarm the administration." A prominent Italian journalist made this statement: "I am certain that if these Italians thought they were really voting communism into power, at least five of the seven million who voted Communist would not do so."

Brinkmanship of this sort not only is dangerous but can misfire. It has been said many times that the best cure for communism would be a Communist regime of short duration. But the trouble is that while it would be comparatively easy to vote Communists into power, no way has yet been devised of voting them out.

THE COMMUNIST ROADBLOCK [8]

Since the end of the last war, the central fact in Italian politics has been the presence here of the biggest Communist party outside the iron curtain. . . . This party has projected an image of itself as Italy's ineluctable destiny: sooner or later, by hook or crook—so millions of Italians have believed—the Communists in this country would come to power.

Of the three ways by which Communists might theoretically seize power—revolution, the Red Army, the ballot—the Italian party has long since formally chosen the third. The "Italian road to socialism," a long but respectable parliamentary road, was invented by Palmiro Togliatti, the party's general secretary; and though no Communist party in the world has yet come to power by that avenue, Togliatti has brought his further along than any other.

For all its misfortunes in recent years—the Hungarian uprising, the current economic boom, Khrushchev's de-Stalinization campaign—the Italian Communist party still . . . [polls 25 per cent of the total vote] and controls nearly half the labor movement (45 per cent and . . . going up). By a multiple series of

[8] From "The Communist Roadblock in Italian Politics," by Claire Sterling, Mediterranean correspondent, *The Reporter*. *The Reporter*. 22:22-6. Ja. 4, '62. Copyright 1962 by The Reporter Magazine Company. Reprinted by permission.

alliances, it can also claim as its own from a third to a half of the Socialists' 4.2 million votes; and alone or with the Socialists, it governs eighteen hundred towns and cities. Its bloc of . . . deputies in Parliament can make any government's life miserable if not unbearable, and in several northern strongholds like Tuscany and Emilia, it *is* the government. Its agitprop workers operate through a network of . . . party cells and numberless auxiliaries—women's and youth groups, summer camps, athletic, movie, and cultural clubs. Its propaganda apparatus includes four daily newspapers, fifty-odd periodicals (covering every field from Marxist theory to women's fashions, sports, the arts, and a children's comic strip on Negro lynchings in America), and a publishing house with outlets in five major and thirty-eight minor cities. . . .

All this is directed by a staff of 8,000 paid national functionaries, 2,500 other paid functionaries in the trade unions, and 20,000 rather underpaid regional agents for the party and its front organizations, on a budget of $25 million a year. Thanks to the . . . defection of several top leaders, the source of these funds is no longer much of a mystery. . . . Most of its commercial income comes . . . from a straight 2 to 5 per cent agent's commission on half of Italy's trade with the Soviet bloc. The take on this averages about $1.5 million a year. . . . Another estimated $1.5 million comes from membership dues, a similar amount from yearly campaigns for the party's official organ *l'Unità*, and yet another similar contribution from Italy's huge cooperative movement, which has been under Communist control since 1947 and regularly turns over half its profits to the party. The balance, close to $20 million, is delivered more or less openly by the Soviet embassy in Rome.

If this makes the Italian party a rather expensive proposition for Moscow, neither Stalin nor Khrushchev (reportedly even more open-handed) has seemed to mind. The party here has always given them their money's worth and it still does even now, when it is showing marked signs of fatigue.

Outwardly, the party seems as flourishing as ever, or nearly so. Though it has never recovered the trade-union majority it lost when it was defeated at Fiat in 1955, it has been steadily inching back; and while its membership has been dropping since 1956, its electoral strength has never stopped rising. . . .

This rather puzzling phenomenon can be explained by several causes. The economic progress of the nation, while truly remarkable, has unevenly affected the various sectors of the economy and the sections of the country. The government's capacity to cope with the nation's major difficulties has been hampered by the fact that the Christian Democratic party has been too long exposed to the corrosion of power and by internal factionalism. Above all, the various Christian Democratic governments, ruling or in coalition with other democratic parties, never had to contend with what might be called a loyal democratic opposition, for the largest of the opposition parties represented not an alternative government but an alternative regime. Actually, the constantly growing Communist vote has succeeded both in weakening the Christian Democrats and in exposing them to the temptations inherent in having to govern with no alternatives.

If the electoral strength of the Communist party has been mounting, so has the economy of the nation and the eagerness on the part of all social groups to enjoy a bigger slice of the national pie. *L'appetito viene mangiando*, the Italians say—appetite comes with eating. The Communists have been riding the wave of the nation's economic improvement and have kept their apparatus going with the up-to-date efficiency of a machine that can almost be run by automation. If a town is struck by fire or flood, Communist cadres are unfailingly first on the scene with hot coffee and blankets. If a peasant needs help in filling out endless legal papers for his pension, he can apply to the local Communist section without waiting for hours in an antechamber or bringing a gift, as Italian tradition requires. . . .

A substantial portion of the party's voting strength results from this kind of combined social work and pork-barreling, particularly in the northern cities that have long been under a Communist regime. In Bologna, for instance, where Communist Mayor Giuseppe Dozza has ruled unchallenged for sixteen years, the prospect of unseating him appalls even the conservative middle class: not only does Dozza run the city beautifully—the party's League of Democratic Municipalities carefully trains city planners, administrators, technicians—but he dispenses patronage so judiciously that his downfall would bring any number of good bourgeois lawyers, accountants, contractors, and commercial suppliers to ruin.

Nevertheless, this has little to do with ideological conviction, or the iron-willed fighting power that makes for a classic Bolshevik party. The kind of Communists who make up that kind of party are rapidly vanishing from Italian ranks. An impressive number have left: nearly 400,000, by official reckoning, since Hungary and Khrushchev's first anti-Stalin report in 1956—but probably closer to a million, since the official figure represents the net loss, allowing for an average of 150,000 new recruits each year. Those who remain have been systematically screened and rescreened, especially in the higher echelons: since 1956, the central committee and the control commission have been twice reshuffled, with nearly two thirds of the old personnel replaced. . . .

The quality of these new leaders is an interesting clue to the party's contemporary role in Italian affairs. Young, cynical, contemptuous of the desperately sentimental Bolsheviks of old, many of them have been drawn to the party primarily by the elemental desire to get ahead. No other party in Italy can offer an ambitious politician such a quick trip up the ladder to political prominence and public esteem, with a large captive audience, a seat in Parliament (at a salary of $800 a month), and a curious sort of homage, one third admiration, two thirds an insurance policy—for who can be sure of what may come?—that is reserved here for the Communist alone. Apart from the prime minister himself, Togliatti is the only politician in the country who is greeted personally and treated to vermouth and cookies by the director of RAI, the Italian radio network, when he appears for a television interview.

Though none of these leaders can match Togliatti, who is matchless at politicking, they are unquestionably able. But all their energies, all their acquired glamor, find their reward in campaigning and in parliamentary maneuver, and here they stop.

No wonder the once fearsome party has grown sluggish and top-heavy. According to the Communists' own publications, only 200,000 party members attend at least one meeting a year, which is to say that 1,528,000 members don't go to meetings at all. As a result, the party's organizational pyramid has been shrinking markedly at the base. Since 1956, it has closed down 16,192 cells, including a third of those that used to function inside the factories; and most of the remaining factory cells exist largely on paper. This is particularly true in the northern industrial triangle, where the party's membership losses have been greatest: 37 per cent in Turin, 27 per cent in Genoa, 22 per cent in Milan. Even in Milan's Brown-Boveri plant, says *l'Unità*, "where the workers' organized force never failed in the blackest years of our history, there is a constant fall in membership." While the workers still make up 37.9 per cent of the party, therefore, they have become an increasingly passive force, led—or pushed—by the intellectuals (0.6 per cent) at the pyramid's top. The action squads of former days are mostly gone. By now, the party must rely on mercenaries for practically every service it requires, from peddling *l'Unità* to scrawling graffiti on city walls; and it is no longer possible for Togliatti to turn on a riot, or even a rally, at will. . . .

This doesn't mean that the Communists here are now incapable of mob action. But, as a former high functionary explains, their disposition to strike or riot has come to depend less on blind discipline than on how they feel personally about the issue at stake. According to this source, for instance, the central committee was baffled . . . [in 1961] by a rash of strikes fomented by some obscure workers in the north, and had immense difficulty in calling them off.

> Even now [he says], the central committee doesn't know why they went out or what they wanted. And that isn't by any means an isolated case. The truth is that the party today could not start—or stop—a general strike merely because it wanted to. As for a revolution, the question is hardly worth discussing.

There was a time when discussion of that question might have been worth while. The Italian party has had three excellent opportunities for a revolution, and each time it has deliberately averted it. The first came just at the end of the war, when, as Togliatti has said:

> There was a situation in Italy in which it would not have been difficult to take power and begin to build a Socialist society. . . The greater part of the population would have followed us. . . . [But] the country was occupied by the American and British armies; an insurrection against these armies would have been politically absurd, and destined to sure defeat.

He did not add that such an insurrection would have been resolutely opposed by Stalin, who flatly told him so.

Stalin never wanted a Communist regime anywhere that was not directly under the control of the Red Army—his main reason for breaking with Tito. Nor did he want to take any risks after the war that might invalidate the Yalta Agreement, which, while leaving the Italian Communists in a capitalistic limbo, gave Stalin all the time he needed to digest his new Eastern European empire. Having noted the Western reaction to the postwar Communist uprising in Greece (whose leader he later dispatched to Siberia), he was anything but eager for a similar Italian adventure.

When Togliatti returned to Italy, therefore, after waiting out fascism and the war in Moscow, he came in the parliamentarian's double-breasted blue suit that has become his uniform. With the only organized party in Italy and millions of enthusiastic sympathizers, with his northern partisans still armed and jubilant in the knowledge that revolution was around the corner, . . . Togliatti announced urbanely that there would be no revolution. The Communists' task, he said, was to "create a progressive and democratic regime" in Italy. "We know how deep the destruction of Italy's social fabric has been," he explained. "If we were to have any other objective, we would fail in our duty to the nation."

His strategy then, and since, was to avoid all frontal attacks and develop a maneuverable mass party which, in coalition with "the more progressive" Socialist and Catholic forces, could achieve power legally; and believing this goal very near—he was already in the provisional cabinet—he left no stone unturned to reach it. In those early years, for example, he not only gave tacit support to the discredited Italian monarchy but even voted to insert the Vatican Concordat in the new constitution. (This overture to the Christian Democrats was a sad failure, since Prime Minister De Gasperi threw the Communists out of the cabinet just three weeks later.) At the same time, Togliatti waged merciless war within his party on "vulgar anticlericalism," "infantile sectarianism," and all the other bad habits of die-hard Bolsheviks.

Despite his efforts, revolutionary conditions persisted. In 1947, a mere incident touched off a semi-insurrection in the north, with tumultuous strikes and riots, and an armed occupation so nearly complete that when Interior Minister Mario Scelba called his Milan prefect on a private line, it was Communist

Central Committeeman Giancarlo Pajetta who answered the telephone. The occupation ended as abruptly as it began. But the north wind blew again, and more strongly, the following summer when a young Sicilian took a shot at Togliatti and nearly killed him. In the resulting outbreak, every major factory in Turin and Milan was occupied, policemen were disarmed, and partisans' roadblocks went up throughout northern and central Italy. Even in phlegmatic Rome, excited crowds were shouting, "*Dacce er via!*"—"Give us the go-ahead!"—to their leaders. The party's reply was solemn: "Citizens, comrades . . . let us pay homage to Togliatti by passing in silence before the gates of the Policlinico, where he lies." The party's revolutionary era ended with this silent homage.

Though Togliatti's hopes for an early electoral conquest were dashed in the elections of 1948, when the Popular Front polled only 31 per cent in the national elections, he did not find the outlook too discouraging. While the front was later disbanded, he was able to keep Pietro Nenni's Socialist party so closely bound to him that he could, in effect, claim nearly 45 per cent of the electorate by 1960; and for all the Vatican's efforts—including a decree of mass excommunication for Communists—he has managed to maintain a broad avenue of communication with the Catholic masses. The Italian Communist party is probably the only one on earth, in fact, that can be said to have "solved" its religious problem: 90 per cent of its members are, if not full practicing Catholics, at least baptized, married, and buried by the Church.

Nevertheless, the Communist tide has both swollen and slowed down. The Italian middle class, growing sleek and confident, is no longer so vulnerable to Communist pressure; many an intellectual, since Hungary, has drifted away from the party; and even the workers, whose aspirations have been keeping step with their pay checks, are beginning to think less about improving the lot of their own class and more about moving a step higher to the middle one.

Togliatti's indispensable ally, the Socialist party, seems finally to be breaking away. The process is far from completed: while Nenni's party has officially severed its ties with the Communists, it is still trying a disengagement maneuver in the trade unions and municipal councils, and at least a third of its organizational apparatus is still in the hands of pro-Communists (many of whom are on Togliatti's payroll). Still, it is doubtful whether the Socialist masses can be counted on any longer to play a role in Togliatti's grand design.

The Communist party is more than adequate in the role Moscow had assigned to it: maybe not to govern Italy but certainly to render it as far as possible ungovernable. This kind of job Togliatti can do admirably. He has managed to keep Italian democracy in a state of constant jitters—not only by what he has done but by what he has led democratic leaders to think he might do. With all the democratic parties combined barely able to muster a majority in Parliament, successive governments have been afraid to seek help from the Right lest an anti-Fascist voter fall into Togliatti's arms—or from the Left lest they themselves fall into his arms. . . .

To harass the government suits Togliatti perfectly, but not all his followers. The notion has dawned on many of them that for the Soviet Union their big party is only a weapon of harassment against the West. The feeling has started spreading that the party's revolutionary radicalism may have become a mere ceremonial, or that at the utmost the party has become a mass of maneuver to be used as a low-priority reserve in the contingency planning of the Soviet Union.

These doubts, slow to mature, did not begin to dawn among the party faithful until 1956, the year when Khrushchev made his first report on Stalin and Red Army tanks rolled into Budapest. Stunned by these events, thousands of Communists could not help wondering . . . what might conceivably happen if the Red Army, on which their last hopes were pinned, should one day roll into Rome. Dissatisfied with Togliatti's reply, 250,000 of them quit the party at once, and others have been doing so ever since. . . .

By all accounts, the odds so far are against Togliatti's losing the reins of leadership. But whether he stays or goes makes comparatively little difference to the party that has so long been molded in his image. The Communist party, even with all its electoral following and its organized or unorganized fellow travelers, is not big enough to conquer power, while it may have become too flabby to try revolution. Still, it is one of the major causes for the chronic unbalance of Italian democracy, one of the main reasons why the government here has frequently, and rightly, been accused of immobilism. The huge Communist parliamentary group has encouraged the fretfulness of over-ambitious marginal men in and out of the majority coalition.

DEMOCRACY IN TROUBLE? [9]

Italy is the only major European country that hasn't efficiently solved the postwar problem of self-government. West Germany is handing on from Adenauer with minimum fuss; even those who dislike Gaullism admit it works in France; and regardless of crises, no one ever doubts the British talent for ruling themselves.

But the vivid, clamorous Italians make scant perceptible progress. Today . . . there is no real administration capable of valid policy commitments. To be sure, the paraphernalia of the state are there: dignified, gentle president; Parliament, cabinet and rather turgid bureaucracy. . . .

The essential trouble is that each of the two real power poles is magnetized by non-Italian currents. One is the brilliantly led Communist party, still closely linked to Moscow. The other is the Christian Democratic party, originally founded at Vatican rather than national behest to fight communism and recreate a stable state. Today its political machine seems fueled more by holy water than by energy.

Under its remarkable first leader, Alcide de Gasperi, it had great initial success. There was but one real choice for Italy—Marxism or democracy. Marxism meant Moscow and, in a strange way, democracy meant anticlerical Washington plus the Vatican. Both Washington and the Vatican made it plain they would never permit a Communist take-over here, licit or otherwise, and openly intervened in at least one election.

Since then, however, Russia's de-Stalinization rid the Italian Communists of embarrassing rigidities without hurting their or-

[9] From "Another 'Catastrophic Perspective'?" by C. L. Sulzberger, foreign affairs columnist, New York *Times*. New York *Times*. p 22. Ag. 9, '63. Copyright by The New York Times. Reprinted by permission.

ganization. A similar loosening of the Vatican monolithic system only served to weaken the Christian Democrats while new papal tolerance seemed to view communism as more respectable. Italy prospered and a big slice of agricultural population moved to the traditionally Marxist industrial cities. Finally, the Kennedy Administration openly approved the experiment here called Opening to the Left—which Eisenhower had discouraged.

Opening to the Left, a slogan that obsesses Italians, refers to a Christian Democratic effort to lure the Nenni Socialists from previous Communist ties, thus building a solid majority while isolating the Communists. So far it hasn't worked.

It is dubious whether Nenni, who seems to covet a chance of returning from the oppositional wilderness, could truly deliver his supporters. Certainly Socialist union members won't quit the Communist-run labor federation and, in provincial elections, the Communists and Socialists still work hand in hand. . . .

The economic growth rate has slowed; inflation mounts; some people transfer savings abroad. There is suppressed fear that, in its efforts to attract Socialist support, the Christian Democratic government may concede too much to Socialist neutralism.

One may even speculate that the Center's famous Opening to the Left could ultimately turn into an Opening to the Right by the Communists, who have so far gained more votes than those who inaugurated the experiment. The Italian atmosphere is leaden with pessimism. One hears increasing talk of an inescapable popular front if the Left-Center alliance fails.

Conservatives compare Rome today with Prague fifteen years ago when the Communists legally voted themselves into power. Italy again approaches that situation once described by Antonio Gramsci, founder of this country's Communist party: a "balance of forces with a catastrophic perspective" that would inevitably lead to dictatorship.

It is less easy than a decade ago for Washington to assert it would not tolerate a Communist Italy, even if brought about by legal means. And Vatican opposition also seems less stubborn in the public mind. Washington has endorsed the Opening to the Left and it is probably too late to contemplate a reversal.

The choice still lies between communism and democracy, although each less rigid. The Center-Left maneuver tries to refurbish the democratic symbol. Should it fail, the next choice might be between popular front and rightist autocracy. Heaven forbid! Italy tried that once.

III. THE ECONOMIC MIRACLE

EDITOR'S INTRODUCTION

The resurgence of the Italian economy since the end of the Second World War has been a phenomenon bordering on the miraculous. When Mussolini's Fascist regime collapsed in 1943, the Italian economy, like Italian democracy, was in ruins. The ravages of war were everywhere, and the future was clouded with uncertainty. Parts of the nation had been heavily damaged during the fighting between the liberating Allied armies and the Nazis. Many highways, bridges, and factories had been destroyed, and the nation's economic base was badly shaken.

That was two decades ago. Today the Italian economy is one of the strongest in the world and has a growth rate nearly double that of the United States. Italian cities are now showplaces of the nation's new prosperity. Products of Italian factories—typewriters, motor scooters, autos, generators, ships—are exported all over the world where they find ready markets. Agriculture is slowly giving way to industry as thousands of Italians leave their farms every month to find jobs in the nation's burgeoning factories. Instead of unemployment, there is actually a shortage of skilled labor; instead of being a borrower, Italy now finds herself a world creditor with a surplus of dollars and gold.

Italians have never been so prosperous—yet there are some dark clouds on the economic horizon: labor troubles and inflation spell possible trouble ahead for the *miracolo economico;* the southern part of the country has not shared in the industrial revolution that has swept the north; and there is still poverty in the midst of great wealth. The articles in this section are designed to highlight the main areas of Italy's economic boom and the problems that lie ahead.

The first article, written by Jane and Andrew Carey for the Foreign Policy Association, examines the Italian economic recovery and the effects of nationalization of certain key industries. Edwin Dale, Jr., foreign economic correspondent of the New York *Times,* deals with the existence of poverty amidst Italy's new wealth, while in the following article Thomas Ottenad of the St. Louis *Post-Dispatch* explains the new confidence Italians have in their rapidly expanding economy. In the fourth article of the editors of *Time* deal with the boom that has transformed northern Italy, while the succeeding article by Walter Lucas is concerned with the threat of inflation. The next article, from the British weekly *The Economist,* scrutinizes Italian labor unions, and in the following article, from *Fortune,* Spencer Klaw draws a portrait of Italy's new business managers, the architects of the *miracolo economico.* Italian agriculture is the subject of Walter Lucas' article from the *Christian Science Monitor,* and in the final article of the section, also from the *Monitor,* Keith de Folo tells what happened when the American supermarket came to Italy.

POSTWAR ECONOMIC RECOVERY [1]

Despite its remarkable economic progress in recent years, Italy is still a relatively poor country. Average Italian per capita income for the past few years has only been about one half that of other Common Market countries and a quarter that of the United States.

Italian industrialization has had to face a variety of hurdles which have slowed its progress. Italy lacks many of the raw materials required by modern industry. Its agriculture must exploit land that is largely mountainous and much eroded, except for the great Po River plain in the north and the few fertile areas along the coast near Naples, and in Apulia and Sicily. The country's long bootlike shape impeded transportation as well as the simplest exchange of goods between different sections of the country.

The political difficulties were no less formidable. The country's late emergence as a unified nation slowed the growth of an agricultural or industrial market of any size. Capital was lacking

[1] From *Italy—Change and Progress,* pamphlet by Jane Perry Clark Carey, former State Department official and assistant professor of government at Barnard College, and Andrew Galbraith Carey, former chief of the Industry Division (for Italy) of the now defunct Mutual Security Administration. (Headline Series no 158) Foreign Policy Administration. 345 East 46th St. New York 17. '63. p 27-37. Reprinted by permission.

everywhere. A single manufacturer could frequently handle all the demand for one product and so was able to develop an effective monopoly. This is one of the important factors accounting for the development of Italy's present-day, gigantic industrial combines—Fiat, Pirelli, Montecatini, Milan-Edison, etc.

In the World War I era of cartels and cartelized thinking, Italian industry continued to evolve. Although Mussolini's autarchic policies and the depression of 1929-1932 interrupted industrial progress, development reached a pre-World War II peak in 1939.

The war left the Italian economy in a disastrous condition: its factories bombed; machinery destroyed, worn out or removed; the morale of the people at low ebb. First UNRRA, then American aid provided funds for emergency rehabilitation, including desperately needed fuel and raw materials. It was the Marshall Plan, however, that provided the real springboard for Italian industrial recovery and triggered the impulse for the economic miracle that began in the late 1950's. From 1946 to 1961 total United States foreign assistance to Italy amounted to $5.6 billion, of which $3.4 billion was economic aid and $2.2 billion, military. American financial aid made possible some of Italy's most modern plants; companion programs of technical assistance acquainted labor and industry with needed new methods and techniques. But in the last analysis, it was Italian hard work, creativeness, a developing entrepreneurial spirit and the ability to capitalize on opportunities that account for Italy's economic renaissance.

The postwar development of Italy's steel industry provides a revealing case history of the forces at work in the country's economic growth. With its two major plants at Genoa and Naples destroyed during World War II, Italy found itself with less than half of its former productive capacity and with outmoded plants that produced high-cost steel. New and modern plants were built with Marshall Plan aid, and were continually enlarged. From 1949 to 1961 steel production increased 4.5 times in volume. Demand is rising so fast, however, that even the 15.8 million-ton capacity projected for 1965 will not be able completely to eliminate imports.

The advent of the European Coal and Steel Community (ECSC) in 1952—of which Italy was a charter member—was a collateral factor contributing to industrial growth. Inasmuch as tariffs on coal, iron and steel trade within the community were abolished, Italian prices for these commodities had to be competitive with those of other ECSC members. This meant lower prices, and these in turn benefited other steel-using industries which were able to curtail some former imports of finished steel. And while the steel output of the six ECSC members increased from 42 million tons in 1952 to over 73 million tons in 1961, Italy's share rose from 8.3 to about 12 per cent in the same period.

One of the important factors in Italy's economic resurgence is the availability of new sources of energy and fuel. With its hydroelectric power developed close to the maximum extent possible Italy is increasingly turning to gas and oil. Most of the oil must be imported, but providentially natural gas was discovered in 1946 in great quantities in the Po Valley. Gas has become the major fuel of the vital Milan-Genoa-Turin industrial triangle and of course saves Italy foreign exchange it would otherwise need to pay for imports of oil and coal. In the last few years natural gas deposits have been discovered at Gela in Sicily and at Ferrandina in Lucania in the south, where they are on the way to stimulating important economic development.

In 1961, natural gas provided 11.5 per cent of Italy's total consumption of fuel and power. Meanwhile, anticipating vastly increased future needs, Italy is planning to use nuclear energy to reduce the growing pressure of demand for existing fuels. One of the original members of Euratom, it is already well along the road to the construction of plants that will use atomic energy to produce electricity. With its new nuclear reactors, Italy is sharing in the research programs of Euratom.

Petrochemicals povide still another success story of Italian postwar development. With an abundance of natural gas, and with supplies of oil available in the Middle East and North Africa, the petrochemical industry has jumped ahead. Ravenna, once the seat of empire but more recently a declining city, has been revitalized, thanks to its location on the edge of the great Po gas fields. In the poverty-stricken areas around the gas fields recently discovered in the south and in the oil fields in Sicily petrochemical plants are springing up and bringing new vitality and growth. The port of Brindisi on the southern Adriatic coast, easily accessible to oil imports, is the location of a new petrochemical center built by Montecatini.

From these petrochemical plants, new products are pouring out—synthetic rubber, plastics, and synthetic fibers. Italy has, in fact, become one of the principal manufacturers of certain types of these products in Western Europe.

Many external factors have helped spur Italian economic development. The fall in the prices of raw materials on the international market after the Korean War came at a propitious time. Western Europe's prosperity stimulated growth. The countries of Western Europe imported more goods from Italy, sent it greater numbers of tourists and offered increasing employment opportunities to its technicians and unskilled laborers.

Finally, the impact of the Common Market, which Italy joined as a founding member in 1957, has been of immense significance. The freer movement of trade, labor and capital provided under the Common Market treaty has been a major stimulus to the Italian economy. Italy's markets have begun to expand to include the 170 million people of the member countries.

Some Italians feared that their country would not be able to adjust to tumbling tariff walls and unrestricted admission of products from other member lands. Italian industry, however, has met the challenge head on. Greater efficiency and new techniques have resulted in cost reduction.

However, the implementation of the Common Market program in the agricultural field promises to bring difficulties to the Italian farmers, as it will to those of some other member countries. But it is perhaps not too optimistic to foresee that in agriculture, as in industry, new techniques will result in increased productivity and cost reduction and make the farmers of Italy more competitive.

Government has played an important role in Italy's postwar economic development. There are several reasons for this—traditional, historical and political. Like many other European countries Italy has long had governmental monopolies in the production of such products as salt, tobacco and quinine. The government has operated railroads and telegraphs for half a century, and has controlled the telephone system since 1955.

Until recently, moreover, Italy has lacked a large confident group of venture capitalists and industrialists ready and able to take business risks. The government has been expected to assist private industries in difficulty or to provide funds for industrial development. Furthermore, the trend toward monopoly in private industry reinforced the trend toward monopoly by government. And long after the death of fascism the influence of the idea of a government-dominated corporative state remained alive. Finally, Communists, Socialists and others left-of-center have continually advocated varying degrees of government ownership and operation of the means of production.

In 1962 the Fanfani government pushed through legislation nationalizing electricity. The press reported that the nationalization was a *quid pro quo* promised by the government in return for Socialist "external" support. But this is certainly not the whole story. Many in the Left wing of the Christian Democratic party and among Social Democrats and Republicans believe that government can meet the anticipated tremendous need for electrical power better than private industry. Some observers think that nationalization will make it possible for the consumer to buy electricity at lower cost. Critics predict prices will have to be increased if the government embarks on a large program of expansion of facilities and if prices reflect true costs. Many businessmen fear that other industries may be next in line for government take-over. . . .

Perhaps the best-known government agency is the National Hydrocarbons Agency (ENI), which was set up in 1953 as a holding company for a multitude of already successful and expanding government-controlled or -owned enterprises. The late Enrico Mattei, one of the most brilliant and controversial personalities of the postwar period, was personally responsible for its far-flung development.

Well known as a Catholic partisan in the Resistance during World War II, Mattei rose to fame soon after the war's end. He was then northern director of the Italian General Petroleum Company (AGIP), which had been founded in 1926 to prospect for oil within Italy. AGIP was so unsuccessful that Mattei was ordered to liquidate it. He disregarded instructions, kept his equipment in the field and his fences mended in Rome and went ahead prospecting. Luck was with him as it was all his life until his untimely end in an airplane accident in October 1962, for in 1945 AGIP struck the first large natural gas field in the Po Valley. Then, as the head of ENI, Mattei triumphed over foreign oil companies and private Italian interests in acquiring a government monopoly on all oil and gas in that area.

Using profits from its gas production, ENI then expanded on a vast scale and now operates a network of filling stations, motels and pipelines throughout Italy and across its borders, as well as industrial plants, petrochemical works, refineries and a fleet of tankers. In 1961 ENI cut the price of gasoline, throwing what appeared to be a bombshell into the Italian oil industry. No great conflagration took place, however, and other oil companies followed suit. The government then reduced taxes. As a result, Italy no longer has the highest priced gasoline in Europe, as it had for many years.

Increasingly important on the Italian economic scene are "mixed enterprises"—financed partly by private capital and partly by the government, but in most cases controlled by the government because it owns the majority of the shares in these companies. The giant government holding company is the Institute for Industrial Reconstruction (IRI). It was established under fascism to bail out financially embarrassed industrial concerns. IRI reaches into the heart of the nation's economic life and participates in nearly 100 separate companies. IRI enterprises produce over half of Italy's steel, four fifths of its iron, a quarter of its electricity; build three quarters of its ships; operate its major shipping lines and its Alitalia airlines; supply its telephone services; run its radio and television stations and four of the largest banks in the country.

Today many IRI industries, such as steel, are making money; but others, like the shipyards, are in the red. Some observers wonder why the government continues to nurse along such ailing industries. One reason given is that it helps combat unemployment.

So important had both IRI and ENI become by 1955 that a Ministry for State Participations was set up to try to keep track of and, it was hoped, to control the many activities of both. However, it has been said that ENI, and to a lesser degree IRI, have occasionally come to control the ministry. For several years before Mattei's death there was an increasing belief among Italians that Mattei and ENI had become too powerful, despite their accomplishments.

The direction of ENI's control in the future and of that within the organization itself are in the lap of the gods since the loss of

Mattei. Whether his empire, a "state within a state," will be reduced in size and scope, particularly in its foreign commitments, and whether ENI will become just another government agency remains unknown as yet. Whatever happens, Italy will not soon see Mattei's like again.

AFFLUENCE AND POVERTY [2]

An age of affluence has dawned in Italy, a land whose poverty is as old as its history.

It is a land where eyes and ears confirm the statistics—where expansion and growth are palpable.

Italy was so far behind that even ten years of very rapid growth have still left her by every test the poorest of the "advanced" countries of Europe. . . .

But a start has been made. No visitor can fail to be dazzled, and sometimes annoyed, by the flashy apartment buildings in and around almost every town, the modern factories already built or in process of construction, the multitude of trucks on the roads, the Atlantic City atmosphere of Lake Maggiore and the northern Adriatic coast or the spectacular new superhighways through the mountains.

The burst of energy is perhaps most striking in Milan, which seems to have more opportunities for sidewalk superintendents than any other city in the world.

The beginnings of the age of affluence have meant a better life for the majority of the 50 million Italians and a tremendous improvement for some. But thus far, for various reasons, Italy's "economic miracle" has found expression more in new physical assets than in the things that most closely affect the everyday life of the working man and his family.

A labor union official in Rome put it this way:

"Of course wages have gone up and unemployment has come down. But in this classic—and belated—capitalist investment boom, I'm afraid the social side has been left behind."

He was alluding not only to the relative slowness with which Italian wages have risen, despite the steep rise in production. He was well aware, too, of such pitiful sights as occur in Turin and

[2] From "Italy Enters the Age of Affluence but Continues to Battle Poverty," by Edwin Dale, Jr., foreign economic correspondent, New York *Times*. New York *Times* p 1+. S. 18, '61. Copyright by The New York Times. Reprinted by permission.

Milan when people from the south arrive by train to seek jobs in these boom towns. The newcomers carry all their possessions in a cardboard box, find homes only in a form of southern "ghetto" and face difficulty even in making themselves understood by the northerners. . . .

But none of these things changes the fact that the "miracle" is occurring. The fruits, judging from all past evidence in other countries, will spread increasingly.

What, then, is the Italian story? What brought about the great advance? What has it meant to the country and its people?

A good place to begin is the tremendous and expanding Fiat automobile plant . . . in Turin. Its 30,000 workers are already turning out 2,500 cars daily, a third for export, and its capacity will reach 4,000 daily in a few years.

None of the men working the endless rows of machines is entirely "typical," but a composite man might add up to the following:

The chances are slightly better than even that he was born in a rural village rather than in Turin. His presence . . . is evidence of what is by far the greatest social consequence of Italy's boom—a rapid migration from farm to city that has brought social strains with economic advances. Italy still has 31 per cent of her labor force on the farm—compared with only 20 per cent in the rest of rich Europe—but it was 50 per cent in Italy a generation ago.

A machine operator classified as semiskilled earns a basic salary of 65,000 lire ($104) a month. In addition he gets about 6,000 lire ($10) for each dependent. Assuming he has a wife and two children, he thus gets a monthly paycheck of 83,000 lire ($133), which is only a little higher than the weekly check of his counterpart in Detroit.

He lives in a fine new apartment built by Fiat with the aid of a special state housing fund. It has two bedrooms, a bathroom and a kitchen and the rent is 19,000 lire ($31) a month. All his medical needs are provided free under a company program.

The worker probably owns a motor scooter, and may perhaps have a baby Fiat that he was able to buy for just under $1,000. He has a television set. He still eats meat only every other day, subsisting mainly on inexpensive spaghetti and bread. His clothing is cheaper than his counterpart's in the United States. This man is the prince of Italian workers. The scale ranges downward from him.

He and other Italian industrial workers have seen their pay-checks—all special benefits included—rise by slightly more than one third since 1953. . . . The national average is now [1961] a little under 50,000 lire ($80) a month, according to the latest estimates.

But the cost of living has risen, too, in the same period, by 17 per cent. Thus "real" wages have gone up only 15 to 20 per cent in the eight years, while industrial production has doubled.

A bank section manager expresses a fairly widely held view:

> Miracle? What miracle? After eleven years in this job I'm getting 90,000 lire a month. The rich get richer, the government is as crooked as ever, and all I see of the miracle is a traffic jam.

The main reason for the relative slowness of wage increases has been unemployment, which has exercised a strong restraining effect. Now, in the industrial region of the north, there is very nearly full employment and wages are starting to rise more rapidly. . . .

By far the greatest human benefit of the miracle has been the reduction in unemployment. There are two different sets of statistics on this, one based on registrations at state employment offices and the other based on a representative sample of the population, as in the United States.

The sample now shows unemployment at about 700,000, while the registration figure puts it twice as much. Informed opinion puts "true" unemployment at 800,000 to 900,000 or well under 5 per cent of the labor force. This compares with a probable "true" figure of about 1.5 million at the beginning of the last decade. Thus unemployment has been nearly cut in half, and the "insoluble" problem of the early postwar period is on the way to being solved.

It is the man who has found a job after not having had one for months or years and the man who has moved from near poverty on the farm to a paying job in the city who have seen their level of life improve most. The biggest jump in personal incomes and consequently in consumption has been among these men rather than among men already working in the cities.

The incomes of those long-time city workers are still anything but high. Consider the cash incomes of the following Romans:

Steel salesman, forty-one years old, eleven years in job, equivalent to $176 monthly.

Bus conductor, thirty-eight, fourteen years in job, $137 monthly.

Clerk in Ministry of Aeronautics, twenty-seven, $96 monthly.

Woman insurance company typist, forty-one, seven years in job, $128 monthly.

These incomes are an expression of the fact that Italy started so far behind the parade. For the first forty years after reunification in 1861 the country scarcely grew at all—the same period when much of the rest of Europe and the United States were roaring into the industrial age.

Then, at the beginning of this century, Italy's latent industrial genius began to show itself. Men like the great Giovanni Agnelli of Fiat and Guido Donegani of Montecatini were adventurous business entrepreneurs on the grand scale. Northern Italy in general caught the industrial spirit of the times and began to show consistent economic advance.

By the outbreak of World War I mechanical industries already had 1,500 factories though they employed only 210,000 workers. The industrial tradition was established and there had never been any doubt of the ability and willingness of Italians to work.

But World War I was a setback. After a period of fairly rapid growth in the 1920's the Great Depression, followed by the "autarchy policies" of the Mussolini regime, which protected nearly all industry from foreign competition, left the country as poor as ever.

World War II dealt what seemed to be the *coup de grâce.* The sheer physical destruction was enormous. One of Italy's three steel mills, for example, was completely destroyed.

It was after World War II that the miracle began. How did it happen?

Men like Vittorio Valetta, the dynamic head of Fiat, and Luigi Einaudi, world-famous economist, who was president of Italy until 1954, deny that there has been any miracle at all.

Signor Einaudi . . . says with a snort:

> Miracle? It has all happened before in other countries. All it took, really, was an act of will in 1947 and 1948 to get the money under control by refusing to give credit to everyone who wanted it—in effect by stopping the printing press.

His basic premise—and that of others—is that the great expansion reflected the classic operation of the profit motive, once United States Marshall Plan aid had covered Italy's immediate recovery needs.

Signor Valetta divides the postwar period into three stages. In the first, Italian industry was still afraid. In the second, beginning about 1950, first efforts at investment and expansion were getting under way. Then by 1955 everyone was getting on the bandwagon.

Since 1956 new fixed investment has represented the astonishing proportion of about 24 per cent of Italy's gross national product, most of it private investment. This is one reason why the consumer has seemed to benefit comparatively little—though he will benefit later.

Others, including Emilio Colombo, brilliant young Minister of Industry, add as a major cause of the nation's economic growth the rapid liberalization of imports from other countries in Europe, although tariffs remained quite high. Italian industry had to modernize or go under and foreign trade expanded rapidly.

Finally, Signor Colombo and others stress the important role played by investments of the state, particularly in the early years of the last decade. There were ordinary public works. There was a big development plan for the south. And perhaps most important, there was the bold investment policy of state-owned industries—particularly in the state-owned part of the steel industry and in the oil and gas operations of Enrico Mattei, controversial chief of the state oil concern.

On all sides much credit for the great expansion of the Italian economy is given to plain hard work. The Italian genius in design and engineering and construction, together with aggressive salesmanship at home and abroad, obviously played a major role. But Italy was never lazy, only backward. The conditions of the last decade have been the first in which her innate industrial ability has had a sustained chance to show itself.

Italy also got one important stroke of good luck. A major reason for her lag behind the rest of the industrial world was her lack of coal and iron for steel-making, to say nothing of other natural resources. But a major change has occurred in the European steel industry.

Lower freight rates, cheap American coal and new iron ore deposits in Latin America and Africa have suddenly made it possible for Italian mills built on the coast to produce steel almost as cheaply as the mills of the Ruhr or of northern France.

A huge new mill is being built by the state-owned steel concern, Italsider, at Taranto, on the coast in the south. By 1965 Italian steel capacity will be up to 12.5 million tons compared with 8.5 million tons now.

Out of it all has come a rate of economic growth that rivals that of West Germany for the most rapid in Europe—far faster in percentage terms than that of the United States in recent years. In the decade ending in 1960, the gross national product in real terms—that is, after allowing for price increases—rose by 5.7 per cent yearly, far higher than in any other period of Italian history.

This compares with just under 7 per cent for West Germany and with 3 per cent for the United States.

Italy now turns out more than 700,000 cars a year. . . . There are now 2.3 million cars on Italy's still inadequate road system, not to mention the trucks. Consumption of durable goods—the ultimate badge of affluence—has doubled since 1953.

Yet Italy still has almost 40 per cent of her people living in the south, Sicily and Sardinia in conditions often close to poverty. Over all she will have to grow for another decade at the present rate to catch up with the present level of incomes, production and living standards of the rest of industrialized Europe.

CONFIDENT ITALY [3]

An American businessman smiled as he glanced out his office window on a sunny, spring day in Rome recently.

"The Italian people," he remarked, "have fallen in love with growth."

[3] From "Confident Italy Expects Economy to Keep on Growing," by Thomas W. Ottenad, writer, St. Louis *Post-Dispatch*. St. Louis *Post-Dispatch*. p 1D+. Ap. 17, '63. Reprinted by permission.

Outside the office the Via Veneto, Rome's most fashionable street, was thronged with smartly dressed, prosperous-looking men and women. Shops displayed chic, Italian-designed clothes and elegant jewelry with beauty and prices that took one's breath away. The traffic jam, as usual, was enormous; the confusion, ferocious; and the scent of success, strong and heavy.

In this street scene there was something youthful and vital about an ancient land that once ruled most of the known world. The attitude was somehow that of a teen-ager, growing fast and full of unlimited confidence about the future.

It was an atmosphere born of success, created by a tremendous surge of power displayed by the Italian economy in recent years, a record that shows growth and more growth at nearly every turn.

Italy's gross national product . . . [in 1962] was nearly double its 1953 level; so was national income. Average income per person in 1961 was 3.5 times what it was in 1948. By the end of 1960, compared with 1953, industrial production had risen by 85 per cent; imports had doubled, and exports had trebled. Italy's holdings of gold and foreign exchange ranked behind only those of the United States, Germany and the United Kingdom.

This was a country where from 1928 to 1948 the income of average Italians had not risen one cent. Yet since World War II the nation has had one of the world's fastest growing economies.

Throughout the 1950's national output rose at a yearly average of 5.9 per cent, two thirds above the American level and fourth fastest among eighteen European nations. In recent years the boom has been even faster. In 1960 the gross national product climbed by 7.1 per cent; in 1961 by 7.9 and . . . [in 1962] by 5.5.

While future growth is likely to be slower than this dizzy pace, both Italians and impartial observers expect it to continue to advance strongly. H. Gardner Ainsworth, the capable and experienced economics counselor for the American embassy in Rome, observed, "Sustained high growth should continue for years and years because there are large-scale demands still unmet here."

Ainsworth predicted annual average growth of between 5 and 6 per cent for the rest of this decade. The significance of such a rate is clearly indicated by the fact that it would double the nation's income in about twelve years.

Despite its history as one of the world's oldest and greatest civilization, Italy in its recent years of advance, has been, in many ways, like a young, underdeveloped nation, because it had so little.

Just how little Italians had is clear from one of Ainsworth's studies. In 1938 average income per person was about $200 a year, a bare 10 per cent higher than its level ten years earlier. Mussolini's grandiose dreams of empire and his repressive Fascist regime had done little for the economy except to clamp tight controls and state ownership on much of it.

By the end of World War II income had dropped even lower. Cut to half its prewar level, it stood at what was probably its lowest point in seventy-five years.

The beginning of postwar reconstruction brought it back up to $200 by 1948, and the impetus of the Marshall Plan yielded further gains by 1953 when most major wartime reconstruction had been completed. Since then the rise has been even faster. By 1961 average income stood at $700, or 3.5 times the 1948 level.

The depressed position from which Italy started has played an important part in its recent big gains. Modern technology, replacing antiquated methods, boosted output sharply. Workers shifted from low-producing agriculture to higher-paying, higher-producing industrial jobs as new factories sprang up. The industrial plant, which had been small, highly protected and rigidly controlled under Mussolini, expanded, pulled down its trade barriers and emerged suddenly on the world scene as a vigorous competitor. Abundant cheap labor and relative price stability also helped.

In the opinion of Ainsworth and other students, including Giovanni Landriscina, economics expert of the Italian Budget Ministry, the government action that contributed most to Italy's outstanding growth has been a continuing policy of high public expenditures and investments.

Between 1951 and 1961, one study showed, government spending rose by 86 per cent, or slightly faster than the gross national product. When public investments, rather than merely operating expenses, are taken into account, the role of the government becomes even more impressive.

Of all the money plowed back into investments in 1961, nearly 40 per cent came directly or indirectly from the government. The rate of both public and private investment has been nearly double that of the United States. Last year 21 per cent of all available resources went into investment.

In typically Italian fashion, the nation's economy is highly individualistic. It seems to disregard most rules, intertwining public and private elements perhaps more closely than any other Western nation. The government plays one of its most significant roles through what are delicately described as "state holdings." These are firms owned either wholly or in part by the central government.

[The] fountainhead of the system is composed of two state holding companies—IRI, the Institute for Industrial Reconstruction, and the better-known but smaller ENI, or National Hydrocarbons Agency. Experts estimate that as much as one third of all production comes from state-controlled firms.

IRI controls more than one hundred operating concerns and exerts a pervasive influence. Through its subsidiaries it controls the entire radio, television, and urban telephone systems; virtually all airline business through the Alitalia commercial line; 80 per cent or more of shipbuilding and pig iron production; more than half of steel output and passenger shipping; one fourth of electric power generation; and one fifth of the banking system.

ENI has five main management firms, around which are grouped seventy-five operating companies, some of which carry on important business abroad. Concentrating principally on oil and gas exploration and production, it also operates a chain of service stations, restaurants, and motels.

The government role in the field of business is a growing one. Last year the electric power industry was nationalized. IRI and ENI together have 325,000 employees. By 1965 the number of workers employed directly or indirectly by state-controlled firms is expected to reach 500,000.

Some of the most important government expenditures have been those in the poverty-stricken southern half of Italy. In an effort to make agricultural and industrial development possible there, the government has undertaken to finance the entire cost of providing roads, water systems and other public utilities for the south. More than 2,000 billion lire (about $3,200 million) in

Federal money has been provided under a fifteen-year program that started in 1950.

Despite its extraordinary growth in recent years, the nation still lags far behind other large Western countries. Using exchange rates for conversion purposes, a study by Ainsworth showed Italy's gross national product in 1961 was about $35 billion.

That was only a little more than one third the total output of the United Kingdom and about one fifteenth of the U.S. level. National income at $27 billion showed about the same ratios.

The extraordinary paradoxes of Italy—where modern automobiles creep slowly through narrow archways in the ancient city wall of Rome, where the impressive ruins of the superbly proportioned Roman colosseum contrast sharply with modern, boxlike apartment buildings splashed with garish colors—extend into the country's economic life.

Although the government has spent and invested heavily, its action, in the view of most impartial observers, was not deliberately designed to stimulate growth. The major aim, rather, was simply to meet accumulated public needs. The threat represented by the Italian Communist party, the largest in Europe outside the Soviet Union, lent political urgency to the task.

There is paradox, too, between economic performance and philosophy. Although Italians think nothing of mixing public and private spending in a strange potpourri, they hesitate at the thought of using other strong government action should their booming economy slip. Italian officials made it plain they would not like to employ the stimulus of a tax cut and budget deficit, now being considered by the United States.

Their reluctance is doubly paradoxical, for the Italian budget has shown deficits regularly for at least forty years. Italian officials point out, however, that the deficits were small and were not deliberate growth devices, but resulted from spending programs that were believed to be needed.

> The Italians really are quite conservative in their economic notions [said one well-informed observer]. Like the United States, their government dislikes tinkering with fiscal measures.
>
> They recall vividly the severe inflation they suffered after the war, and they don't want to risk anything that might lead to it again. Besides, with the boom they have had, they haven't needed tax cuts or other stimuli.

The Italians have jumped on the economic planning bandwagon that has been rolling through much of Western Europe recently. A government commission has been at work on an initial report aimed at establishing a planning system. . .

Informed sources expect eventual development of a rather limited system of long-range economic projections and forecasts, but without the detailed production targets that mark the French economic planning system.

Full of vitality and bursting with confidence, Italians are looking to the future without worry. Although creeping inflation has been apparent for about eighteen months—the cost of living rose 5 percentage points last year and salaries climbed 20 per cent for government workers and an average of about 15 per cent in private industry—most Italian officials see little serious danger ahead.

In love with growth, Italy expects to keep right on growing for some time to come.

ITALY'S BOOMING NORTH [4]

Each opening night during the opera season, Milan's Via Manzoni is transformed from a bustling commercial street to a river of wealth and elegance. Bumper to bumper, a seemingly endless line of Mercedes, Alfa Romeos, Lancias and Maseratis inches toward the Piazza della Scala, their high-powered engines being raced by traffic-frustrated drivers. Pulling up before La Scala's neoclassic façade, the cars discharge their cargoes—usually an Italian businessman, resplendent in white tie, and his bejeweled wife, dressed in a Fontana, Capucci or Dior.

Milan's opulence is no sudden sparkle or passing phenomenon. The city is the dynamic fountainhead of the biggest, most sustained comeback that any European nation has made from World War II ashes. Germany has had its economic miracle, and France its postwar resurgence; both are still prospering but at a slightly slower pace. North Italy has sustained its boom. In Milan the Gothic finials of the renowned *duomo* now have to fight for recognition against a skyline of striking new skyscrapers. From the Piazza del Duomo rises the bedlam that only Italian traffic can generate. In front of the cathedral's stately bronze

[4] From article in *Time*. 79:72-9. Ja. 12, '62. Courtesy *Time;* copyright Time, Inc., 1962.

doors Milan is digging an entrance for its new subway. Everywhere Milanese businessmen move at dogtrot pace in a furious pursuit of profits, and lavish restaurants, such as Giannino, have geared their cuisine and prices to help them spend it.

Not only the businessmen prosper. Milan's workers are the industrial elite of Italy. Per capita earnings have leaped 56 per cent since 1952 to $1,000 a year, which in actual purchasing power amounts to much more. Milan's 1.5 million people pay 26 per cent of the taxes—and grumble as if it were 100 per cent. And all over north Italy—the flaring top quarter of the boot that lies above Florence—workers can now own the refrigerators and television sets they produce. . . .

Italian industrial production, still largely concentrated in the "iron triangle" of Milan, Turin and Genoa, has doubled in the past eight years. So avidly does the rest of the world gobble up Italian products that the nation's balance-of-payments surplus is the envy of the United States Treasury. Buoyed by these achievements, north Italian businessmen, who once argued that they could hold their home markets only with the help of protectionism, today swagger forth on a Common Market invasion of the rest of Europe with all the self-assurance of the Caesars of old.

As always, north Italy is outpacing the rest of the country. The arid south, despite all the Italian government and United States aid money poured in, is still primarily a land of hunger and hopelessness. In startling contrast gleams the prosperity of north Italy, which has replaced the United States as the near and visible promised land in the dreams of impoverished Sicilians and Calabrians. "California begins at Milan," runs the current folklore of south Italy and each day hundreds of southerners board northbound trains to seek the living wage they cannot find at home. . . .

At the end of World War II, most of north Italy's industry lay in ruins, and even to regain the modest prosperity of prewar years seemed a task of decades. The resurgence came much quicker, and for three reasons:

United States Marshall Plan aid of $3.5 billion to Italy—a substantial part of which went to rebuild the north, where there was much more industry that was worth rebuilding.

The tough fiscal policy of the late President Luigi Einaudi, which prevented runaway inflation.

Discovery of methane in the Po Valley, which has given Italian industry a cheap domestic fuel source to stoke its industrial boom.

These strokes of good fortune were converted into "the Italian miracle" by the energy and imagination of north Italian businessmen and the industry of their employees. Unlike the committee-minded U.S. businessman, the Italian chief executive is a free-wheeling autocrat who bases his decision far more on intuition than on the promptings of scientific management.

Probably no Italian industrialist shouldered his way to U.S. attention with more of a jolt than the late Adriano Olivetti. An intense idealist with a Left-trending political philosophy, Olivetti was looked askance at by many other Italian businessmen who argued that what really kept the Olivetti Company going was the sober, steadying hand of financial wizard Giuseppe Pero, . . . now the company's chief executive. Yet, for all his quirks, Olivetti was a marketing genius, who by introducing the sophisticated "Italian look" in office machines, built a family business into an international concern and just before his death . . . startled the business world by acquiring Connecticut's faltering Underwood Corporation in the first major take-over of a U.S. firm by foreigners since World War II.

In Italy, Olivetti's influence never approached that of . . . Vittorio Valletta, . . . managing director of the Fiat automobile empire, which now builds 80 per cent of the 600,000 cars produced in Italy each year and is a major producer of steel, locomotives, marine diesel engines and aircraft. A courtly ex-accountant who rebuilt Fiat from World War II rubble, Valletta led the company to its present near monopoly in Italy partly by taking advantage of a prohibitive tariff on foreign cars. Now that the Common Market is about to change all that, Valletta has moved to keep his hold on the home market with long overdue price cuts, simultaneously has launched an expansion program designed to double Fiat's production and flood Europe with Fiat's smallest cars, the two-cylinder 500 and four-cylinder 600, which undercut Volkswagen in both size and price.

Second in power only to Valletta in Italian private industry is . . . Count Carlo Faina, chairman of the giant Montecatini chemical complex. Despite an aristocratic heritage—he holds a long-standing title granted by Pope Pius IX and confirmed by the

Italian royal family—Faina joined Montecatini thirty-five years ago as one of 360 applicants answering a want ad. Assigned to rebuild the chemical complex after the war, he defied stockholder opposition by multiplying the outstanding shares in order to obtain new capital. Now, with sales of $600 million a year, Montecatini slugs it out internationally with the likes of Du Pont and Britain's Imperial Chemical Industries, and in the Italian market has a reputation for slashing prices until a rival is forced to give up the fight.

No less deadly a competitor is . . . Franco Marinotti, . . . boss of Snia Viscosa, Italy's biggest producer of synthetic textile fibers. Marinotti, who preaches a cold-blooded business philosophy ("Gratitude is a sentiment possessed mainly by dogs"), did his postwar rebuilding without a cent of United States aid. Despite this self-imposed handicap, he pushed Snia into the front rank of industry by automating to cut costs and by instituting a research program so successful in turning up new fibers that, as he boasts, even the U.S.'s Allied Chemical Corporation has signed up to produce Snia's caprolactam, raw material for nylon. As head of one of the world's largest exporting companies, Marinotti brushes aside talk of Common Market challenges. Says he with a grim: "I've always been in the Common Market."

Like Marinotti—who paints passable landscapes under the name "Francesco Torri"—many a north Italian businessman takes as his personal hero that versatile Renaissance genius, Leonardo da Vinci, and like Da Vinci is not deterred from any enterprise by lack of experience. A prime example is Count Gaetano Marzotto, . . . whose family-owned Marzotto Textile is Italy's biggest wool spinner and producer of readymade clothes. Several years ago, enraged by an all-night bout with bedbugs in a Sicilian hotel, Marzotto set out to build his own hotels in Italy's remote places. Clean, simple and inexpensive, the improbably named "Jolly Hotels" were such a success that the Marzottos now have fifty-one of them, the biggest privately owned hotel chain in Italy.

Ferdinando Innocenti . . . is another who combines restless curiosity with shrewd economic sense. One day before World War II, Innocenti, then a small-time maker of steel pipe in Milan, bumped his head on a wooden scaffolding. This, in Da Vinci style, led him to develop the lightweight steel scaffolds now standard the world over. After the war, he bent his tubes into a motor scooter frame and, with his Lambretta, rode the crest of Italy's pent-up demand for cheap transportation. Next, spotting Italian industry's growing need for tools, he began producing heavy machinery and giant electric steel-making furnaces. Recently, to keep up with the middle-class Italian's desire to graduate from two-wheeled transportation to four, Ferdinando, with his son, Luigi, took Innocenti Company into assembling British Motor Corporation's Italian-styled Austin A-40.

Such versatility and drive has enabled north Italy's businessmen to resist, and sometimes overcome, the Italian government's forage into political and economic fantasy. Saddled with a near-medieval tax system that makes an honest declaration of income an invitation to bankruptcy, and perennially endangered by the temptation of Italy's ruling Christian Democratic party to make a deal with the powerful Nenni Socialist party at the expense of free enterprise, Italian businessmen live under a constant state of siege. In the postwar years they fought the threats of Communist unions to take over their companies by handing out paternalistic fringe benefits with a lavishness no U.S. firm would dream of. (After touring the sports grounds, libraries, kindergartens, social center and free medical facilities that Olivetti provides at its Ivrea headquarters, an English visitor dryly remarked: "I assume that the fact that you also produce office machines is pure coincidence.") The results have been mixed: north Italian workers no longer support Communist political strikes, but they go right on electing Communist union leaders as the best economic goads to management.

Even without Communist unions, the north Italian executive must operate in a wondrously mixed economy where there is already more government ownership of industry than in any other country outside the Communist bloc. Born under Mussolini's fascism during the depression, the government-run Institute for Industrial Reconstruction (IRI) owns 30 per cent of all outstanding stock in Italy, controls 350 companies ranging from the nation's largest banks to the Alitalia air service. The busy port of Genoa, whose shipments have tripled to 44 million tons since 1953, is dominated by IRI's Ansaldo shipyards, which built the IRI-operated luxury liners *Cristoforo Colombo* and *Leonardo da Vinci*. . . .

But even where the government is strongest, north Italy's private industry manages to flourish. Though the state produces 55 per cent of Italy's steel, Milan's Falck Steel succeeds by specializing in high-grade alloys. Periodic talk of nationalization of the electric power industry fails to faze ramrod-backed Giorgio Valerio, . . . managing director of Italy's largest utility, the Edison Group. Snaps Valerio: "We've doubled output in ten years, and we're still going ahead. Politicians are conservatives. We industrialists, we are the revolutionaries."

Most Italian businessmen seem to share Valerio's disdain for "those bureaucrats in Rome." After Olivetti's Underwood takeover, one industrialist exulted "Americans used to come here as if they were visiting Black Africa, but they've learned a thing or two." To a man, north Italian businessmen dislike the "Italian miracle" phrase that the Italian press began to use some years ago. Says Leopoldo Pirelli, . . . third generation of his family to run the huge (1961 sales: $220 million) Pirelli rubber company: "There's more perspiration than is normally involved in a miracle." The secret lies far closer to hand, in industrial imagination, high skills, hard work, aggressive ambition. Perhaps the finest result of the north Italy boom is the fact that, after the long years of fascism and the humiliation of military defeat, Italy's national self-respect has been restored and is increasing by the works of its own people.

INFLATION THREAT [5]

If it is not the workers in the railroad or the engineering industries who are striking or threatening to do so, it is the textile workers, the milkmen, the doctors and lawyers, or the state employees—and now, just when school and university examinations are due, the teaching professsion has decided to strike if its demands are not met in full.

Perhaps this is all a part of the price which Italy has to pay for its prosperity and its state approaching full employment—at least for skilled or semiskilled workers.

It is certainly a sign that the present growing inflation is making a lot of people discontented with their rewards for labor, measured in terms of what they will buy.

[5] From "Italy Faces Inflation Threat," by Walter Lucas, free-lance writer. *The Christian Science Monitor* (Eastern edition). p 12. Je. 13, '62. Reprinted by permission.

It is also a growing awareness that the greatly expanded economic cake is not being shared evenly.

This is not, however, something that is peculiar to Italy; France and Germany are having their wage troubles too, and this seems to be a common feature in most countries of Western Europe where economic growth has been the greatest.

Be that as it may, as far as Italy at least is concerned, the result is a rise in industrial costs and prices, which for a country like this, whose economy has suddenly become to a large degree dependent upon exports, is a serious matter.

Wage claims are one thing; strikes to enforce these claims are another. These have been growing in frequency in Italy.

During 1961, 58 million working hours were lost by strikes. Measured in terms of production and productivity, this is serious. . . .

Ten years or more ago Italy was in a worse strike state, but then the reasons were mostly political, the result of Communist agitation. Today they are in the main economic—for higher wages.

For the moment, the most damaging wage pressures are in the various sectors of the civil service—in fact among people whom one does not expect to agitate, such as lawyers, doctors, and schoolteachers. These perhaps have more reason to make demands than any other category of worker, since by and large they have been left behind in the wage-price race.

Perhaps too they have been encouraged to make their claims by the coming into power of a left-of-center government. One which might be more amenable to their demands and less determined to resist them.

There are all manner of other pressures which are closing in on the wage structure. Although there are still 1.3 million registered unemployed in Italy—the majority are agricultural workers who as yet are unsuitable for absorption in industry—this figure is not so alarming as it may seem at first sight.

Nor does it dispose of the claim of a shortage of labor in many economic sectors. In fact, in these days it is not uncommon to find advertisements in foreign newspapers and periodicals appealing to Italians abroad to return home.

Already there has been some response to these, in particular from South American countries where the thousands of postwar emigrants in some cases have found conditions even worse than they were at home.

This shortage of skilled and semiskilled workers gives strength to wage claims. But there is, too, the pressure from industrial workers in northern Italy, especially, to bring their wages in line with those in similar employment in other Common Market countries. Then again the workers in the south are agitating for national wage levels which will put them on a par with their fellow workers in central and northern Italy where prosperity is greatest.

With all this pressure from so many quarters many people are wondering whether the government will be able to hold the wage line, at least within some limit in relation to productivity, and avoid being swept into the wage-rise race. If it cannot do this, there is the prospect of the economic gain of the past decade being diluted in an inflationary flood.

The governor of the Bank of Italy, Dr. Guido Carli, . . . warned of dangers ahead if the government did not exercise extreme prudence. And he was not only referring to wage matters but to the major program of economic and social development which the government has in mind and seems to be set upon carrying out.

This will require vast sums for its implementation. This could put further pressure on the price structure and give an additional push toward inflation.

As Dr. Carli said, there was a real danger in all this to the monetary stability which was a key factor to Italy's future prosperity and economic development.

The tendencies now in motion in Italy could have internal and external effects if they are not checked. The question of whether they can or will be checked is one of the preoccupations of many of the leaders of private enterprise.

They see a combination of the pressure on the wage scale without an equivalent increase in productivity, higher taxation to pay for some of the public expenditure contemplated, and greater borrowing, all three of which could, they contend, bring a deterioration of the present trends.

Some members of the present government are aware of the dangers in the situation, but there are strong pressures from the political Left to carry out in full the program outlined, regardless of the financial consequences.

In the meantime, it can be said that prices and the cost of living continue to climb. . . .

Though this is a bad prospect for Western Europe as a whole, it does have its significance for the United States and can in some way contribute toward helping America's balance-of-payments position, providing the United States costs remain more or less stationary, as they have been for the past four years.

ITALIAN TRADE UNIONS [6]

For nearly forty years Italian industry had lived in a hothouse where the temperature was kept up by the enormous pressure of manpower. Industries, on the plea that they would otherwise have to turn away workers and so add to the chronic unemployment, were able in many cases to pass their liabilities on to the state. The Institute of Industrial Reconstruction acted as a shock absorber, and a system grew up based on high returns for limited output, with risks more or less guaranteed by the state.

This static system was suited to the closed economy of the Mussolini period, but under the impact of new conditions it broke down. During the last ten years—and most decisively between 1955 and 1960—a new dynamic seized Italian industry. It was the result partly of technological innovations, partly of new market conditions, including the advent of the Common Market. But, in great measure, it was the product of new ideas among the political leaders about the function of state industries, thanks in large part to the impulse given to the ENI group (the National Hydrocarbon Corporation) by Signor Enrico Mattei. The rapid expansion of the last few years has not wiped out unemployment; in a sense the problem is more acute than ever, because masses of unskilled labor are pouring into the towns. But highly skilled workers are definitely in short supply.

The younger generation, especially the young people from the technical schools, are keenly alive to the new conditions. Boys trained in the Fiat workshops, for instance, are finding better-paid jobs outside Fiat. Both management and unions have to grapple

[6] From "Italian Labour Out of Step." *The Economist*. 200:48-9. Jl. 1, '61. Reprinted by permission.

with the fact that, for the first time, large numbers of men are entering Italian industry who are not afraid of losing their jobs. Among workers in the most progressive industries, too, the feeling has spread that labor has a right to share the increased profits from technological improvement. The unions no longer oppose dismissals on principle, but claim instead that for every workshop closed a new one must be opened. When Signor Vittorio Valletta, the chairman of Fiat, says, "Once a man joins Fiat we should like never to dismiss him," he is speaking in terms of the conditions of the past—though, to do him justice, the "professor" has an eye to the future when the ascending curve of Italy's motor industry may flatten.

At present the new state of affairs obtains in a few privileged sectors like engineering and steel. Territorially the change affects the industrial triangle of Milan, Genoa and Turin. Its symptoms are the recent protracted strike of the electrical engineering workers in Milan—where strikes have previously always been short and intermittent; the strikes at the Ansaldo shipyards and Breda, one at Alfa Romeo, and the latent unrest at Fiat, where the management is asking the workers to accept a seasonal distribution of working hours which would introduce a fifty-two-hour week for five months of the year.

With its 74,000 workers and its 19,000 office employees, Fiat has the biggest payroll of any single Italian undertaking. After the war its shop steward elections became a barometer of union strength in the country, but in 1955 Fiat succeeded in isolating FIOM (the metal workers' union affiliated to the Socialist and Communist federation, CGIL), and the older union suffered a crushing defeat, to the benefit of the Christian Democrat CISL. Since then trade union affairs at Fiat have followed a pattern of their own. For several years the Catholic union predominated, until it split and gave birth to a "house union" not affiliated to any national federation. In 1960 this *sindicato aziendale* topped the list, but this year it was beaten by the Social Democrat UIL. These fluctuations illustrate the way management plays off one union against another, withdrawing its support when any union grows too strong. But the new fact at Fiat is the appreciable recovery of FIOM. . . . The Communist-Socialist union is not represented among the office staff, but among the workers alone it has stepped forward to first place with 29.6 per cent of the votes, and this in spite of the fact that Fiat does not allow delegates from this union to sit at the table when it negotiates with the other unions. The irony of this is that, of all the five unions at Fiat, the Socialist-Communist metal workers' union is the only one strong enough to discuss, or at least to appreciate, the reasons for the fifty-two-hour week.

FIOM's leaders claim that the election results . . . denote a strengthening of trade union conscience in the workers. Fiat itself points ont that the "Communist" union has advanced in the workshops where new young workers are being engaged. . . .

This does not mean that FIOM, or any of the unions, is sitting pretty. The bargaining power of labor in certain sectors has increased, but the Italian unions are intrinsically weak. They have no strike funds. Their finances are precarious (FIOM with 210,000 members has a budget of £36,000 [$100,800] a year). They depend too closely on the political parties from which they emanate, and they are bitterly divided between the three political federations. In spite of these inherent weaknesses, the Socialist-Communist and the Christian Democrat federations have each set up competent research units and their influence upon Italian economic development is considerable; but it is exercised at a political rather than a trade union level, through Parliament or through organizations such as the National Council of Economy and Labor. Both the Catholic and the Socialist-Communist federations believe that the function of trade unions is not merely to defend the workers' interests against managements, but to put pressure on the government in favor of particular industrial (or agricultural) development policies. Thus FIOM claims that its job is to get industry to produce more production goods and fewer consumer goods. It complains that the large output of utility cars affects the entire economy, and makes the government spend on motorways money that ought to be invested in schools. These criticisms (of Fiat) are tempered by the fact that the Socialist-Communist union has no wish to crush Turin's major industry and by the genuine admiration of its leaders for Signor Valletta as a great industrialist. FIOM also wants the numerous state-owned industries grouped under the Institute of Industrial Reconstruction and the National Hydrocarbon Corporation to be used as pilot industries both as regards production policies and trade union relations. These directives, shared on the whole by the Christian Democrat federation, have certainly influenced government policies over the last two years—witness the steel foundry going up at Taranto, and the ENI foundry at Bari.

There is no closed shop in Italy, and in most sectors union members are less than a third of the total number of workers. The two non-Communist federations, the Christian Democrats and the Social Democrats, enjoy the advantage of some discrimination by management in their favor, but in the long run such favors are a source of weakness, for they generally entail concessions. Thus the Christian Democrat federation lost ground in the last Fiat elections partly because it had agreed to defer the agitation against the fifty-two-hour week. In the last analysis trade unionism in Italy is as strong as the Socialist-Communist CGIL, and no stronger. The old federation sets the tone. This is not to criticize the Christian-Democrat federation. The Catholic unions have a tradition and, were it alone in the field, CISL could probably be tough. But rivalry enervates the weaker federations, while ostracism, at least in the new conditions of the labor market, strengthens the Socialist-Communist federation.

Between management and unions stands the government, in the person of the young and very able Christian Democrat minister of labor, Dr. Fiorentino Sullo. He believes that big industry must learn that labor relations are not purely a matter for the two sides. There is also the law, and in Italy the law assumes that labor is always the weaker party and will not allow it to contract away its rights. He admits, however, that Italian labor legislation is full of lacunae; an article of the constitution and a law of 1923 are almost all there is to go on. Signor Sullo has, therefore, invited industry and the unions to thrash out a new labor code to define all matters concerning the drawing up and application of collective contracts. Such a code was laid down in Denmark in 1899 and is still valid. In Italy it will take months of patience. But Signor Sullo says the important thing is to reach an agreement while industry is expanding. The lack of a recognized labor code could be serious should recession follow the Italian "miracle."

ITALY'S BUSINESS MANAGERS [7]

A young Milanese business executive, wearing horn-rimmed glasses and a beautifully tailored blue-gray suit, recently undertook to explain his political views to an American visitor.

> In Italy, I am a radical [he said]. A moderate radical, I suppose, but a radical. What else can I be? This is not the United States. We have had no Theodore Roosevelt, no Progressive Era, no New Deal. Instead, we had fascism. What we want for Italy is what you already have in the United States. We want a system in which business makes it possible for more and more people to buy the goods it produces. That's the modern way of capitalism, isn't it? When we have this, *then* we will be conservatives.

By "we" the young executive meant Italy's new and rapidly growing class of professional managers. Its members are most heavily concentrated in the booming industrial cities of northern Italy, notably in Milan, Turin, and Genoa. They are also to be found building plastics plants in the Soviet Union, negotiating oil concessions in the Middle East, and selling steel-rolling mills in South America. Their numbers and their rising influence are evidence of fundamental changes that are taking place in Italian business. But the new professional managers are not simply the agents of change; they are also its advocates. They are concerned with changing, not only the way Italian business is run, but the climate in which it operates. They tend to have strong views on, for example, the need for educational reform, the role of the Italian government in the country's economic development, and how to mitigate the ferocity of the class struggle in Italy. On such issues they generally stand a good way to the left of the owner-managers of family firms, who, until just recently, have dominated Italian business life.

In most of Western Europe, as in the United States, the career executive who manages business enterprises he does not own is by now a familiar figure. In Italy, however, professional managers were almost unknown before the onset of the celebrated "Italian miracle"—the astonishing burst of industrial energy that has doubled Italy's output of manufactured goods in the past eight years. Management by professionals is as new to Italy as

[7] From "The New Italian Managers," by Spencer Klaw, free-lance writer. *Fortune*. 66:96-101+. D. '62. Courtesy of *Fortune* Magazine; copyright Time Inc., 1962.

Milan's new skyscrapers, from which the managers may be seen emerging each evening to confront the ghastly traffic jams that, like the skyscrapers, proclaim the country's new prosperity.

Only ten years ago, graduates of the leading Italian engineering schools were hard put to find a job of any kind that paid a decent wage. Today, competition for managers, or manager candidates, is so fierce that a student at, say, Milan's Polytechnical Institute may receive half a dozen attractive offers from corporate recruiters even before he has begun his final year. An engineer who is the son of a professor or a civil servant can reasonably hope to make, after four or five years in business, a higher salary than his father has ever earned. Students taking their degrees in law, economics, or philosophy and letters, who once would have scorned a business career—and would not in any case have been able to find a business job—are now being signed up in increasing numbers, as sales executives, or as members of the burgeoning public relations and personnel departments of big Italian companies.

Professional managers are not yet as solidly entrenched in Italy as in the United States, of course. . . . The family firm is still the prevailing form of enterprise, and even some of the biggest Italian companies are run like medieval baronies. In a recent book called *Speaking the Language Like a Native,* the Irish-Indian author Aubrey Menen describes a call he paid in Milan on Count Edoardo Visconti, head of the big pharmaceutical firm of Carlo Erba.

> My appointment was filtered through secretaries who spoke in the subdued tones of courtiers [Menen writes]. I was received at the headquarters of the concern by what seemed a small army of uniformed attendants. I rose in a gold elevator to an antechamber filled with secretaries and other functionaries . . . there was a flurry of ushers at the door and the chief secretary said to me: "*He* is coming."

But there is no doubt that Italian industry is changing. The enormous expansion of industrial output has led, inevitably, to a sharp rise in the number of big firms. At the same time, many of these firms have become big exporters. Between 1949 and 1961 exports of manufactured goods from Italy rose by 450 per cent, and Italian-made computers, machine tools, and even steel are now being sold in foreign markets where few Italian products other than olive oil and Chianti had ever been seen before. The rapid expansion, often coupled with the need to meet efficient foreign competition, has compelled more and more Italian companies to hire and train professional managers, and to give them authority and independence. . . .

What sort of men are Italy's new managers? To begin with, they are highly educated. Although low-level supervisory jobs in Italian industry are often filled with men who have finished their schooling at a technical institute, it is rare to find a *direttore,* or executive, of a big company who is not addressed as *Dottore* or *Ingegnere,* signifying that he is a graduate of a university or engineering school. "We have no barriers against the non-university man," Dottore Fernando Menzocchi, an executive vice president of Lepetit S.p.A., a pharmaceutical firm with headquarters in Milan, remarked not long ago. Then he tried, in vain, to think of a man who had risen to high executive level from the ranks, and added: "Of course, we have to be realistic. It is terribly important in Italy to be a *dottore.* A man who doesn't have a degree is very apt to develop an inferiority complex when he's thrown together with men who have."

Requiring a university education as a prerequisite for an executive career means one thing in the United States and quite another in Italy. The universities of northern Italy, where the new managers are usually recruited, make much stiffer demands on their students than do most American colleges. (Italian engineering schools are particularly demanding, some students taking six or seven years to get their degrees). Also, to get into a university an Italian must first graduate from a *liceo,* where he will have received a rigorous and severely classical education in Latin, Greek, art, history, modern languages, philosophy, Italian literature, mathematics, chemistry, and physics.

The Italian executive, having survived this ordeal, is obviously a man of intelligence. In addition, even when his higher education has been in mathematics, science, and engineering, he is likely to be what Europeans call a man of culture. He deals easily with abstractions, has a strong sense of history, and while he would not necessarily classify himself as an intellectual, he belongs, unlike many American businessmen, to an upper-middle-class world of people who read books, go to concerts, and like to argue about ideas. More than his American counterpart, he is apt to regard himself as a member of a relatively small national elite.

Most Italian managers, indeed, were *born* into an elite. Shell Italiana recently made an investigation of the social origins of Italian leaders in various walks of life, and found that only 0.6 per cent of the business executives in its sample were sons of manual workers. Eighty per cent were sons of lawyers, doctors, landowners, government officials, teachers, merchants, or businessmen, and 90 per cent described their families as having been at least in comfortable circumstances. The fact is that only a small minority of Italians have the means to send their sons to a *liceo* and to a university, and thus qualify them for an executive career.

While it recruits its managers principally from the sons of the old Italian elite, Italian business has succeeded, in general, in getting the most able and energetic of the crop. Even when their antecedents are distinctly upper class, young men in north Italy, and particularly in Milan, show no prejudice against making money, and there is none of the feeling, still strong in upper-class English families, that business is a suitable occupation only for those not bright enough to do anything else. It is true that Italian university graduates are reluctant to get into direct selling. "They all want to sit at a desk and work with books and papers," a young personnel manager observed recently. (His own desk was littered with papers and books, including a copy of *The Affluent Society.*) "It gives them the illusion that they are really still at the university." But executives of the Olivetti company, which hires from fifty to a hundred university graduates each year, and makes them spend eight months or so selling adding machines and typewriters, say that resistance to this kind of training is steadily diminishing.

In any case, the energetic young graduate who wants to make a good living has little choice other than to make it in business. There are no big corporate law firms competing for the services of young Italians with law degrees. The civil service, which has great prestige in England and France, pays miserably in Italy, and is looked down on in the industrial north as a career suited mainly to languid Neapolitans. There is little possibility, either, of the sort of high-paying academic career, increasingly familiar in the United States, in which teaching, consulting, and sponsored research are combined. A man who is willing to take his licks as an Olivetti salesman can expect that, if he shows promise, he will be earning as much as most full professors within four or five years. . . .

An Italian bent on a career in management does not have to go to work for a big company. He can choose a smaller one whose owner has decided he can no longer run the whole show himself. A company in this transitional phase is usually prepared to pay a young engineer a much higher salary than one of the big companies, and it offers him an opportunity to begin his career close to the top of the managerial hierarchy. But the opportunity involves some risks. Family ties are extremely powerful in Italy, and the proprietor of such a company, while talking the language of professional management, may turn out to be far more demanding of absolute loyalty to himself and his family than of professional competence.

> He is still essentially dynastic but he is insecure [Franco Ferrarotti, a well-known Italian sociologist, has written], . . . because aliens are in the family now for purely professional reasons. Are they going to be reliable? Can one trust them? But one *must* trust them and delegate decision-making power to them if the company is to survive. . . . This setting is rarely successful for the professional manager.

As one might expect, the big companies are more hospitable to the professional manager, and they set the tone of managerial life in Italy. The new managers make little distinction between big companies that are privately owned and those in which the Italian government is the controlling stockholder. In the state-controlled companies, which employ more than 300,000 persons all told, people are sometimes hired, and decisions are sometimes made, in response to political pressure. But a number of the state enterprises, notably the huge Italsider steel company . . . have the reputation of being excellently managed. And most young managers seem to feel that, on the whole, political nepotism is no larger a problem in the big state-controlled companies than family nepotism is in the big private companies.

The management of these companies has been very strongly influenced by American practices. During the 1940's and early 1950's, when Italian industry was getting back onto its feet, hundreds of young Italians were sent to the United States . . . to study American techniques—of organization and marketing as well as production. Management-training courses in Italy are modeled on courses given in the United States, and Italy's first graduate business school, IPSOA (Instituto Post-Universitario per lo Studio dell'Organizzazione Aziendale), which was established in Turin in 1952 by Olivetti, Fiat, and the Turin manufacturers' association, was staffed for many years by American professors of business administration.

Despite the American influence, an Italian company typically has fewer managers than a comparable American company. It may, indeed, have only half as many. One reason is simply the shortage of qualified men, especially in engineering. In 1960, for instance, when the personnel department of Montecatini, Italy's biggest chemical company, asked each division of the company how many young chemical engineers it needed, the sum exceeded the total number due to graduate that year from Italian universities. Another reason is that directors of Italian firms have not entirely shaken off their pre-"miracle" mode of thinking about executives. While they have been willing to spend big sums on apartment houses and swimming pools for their workers, and more recently for public relations (the office of the chief of public relations at Fiat's headquarters in Turin is roughly the size of a tennis court), they are apt to be deeply suspicious of any proposal to enlarge the company's executive establishment. . . .

Another big difference between Italian and American managers lies in the way they treat the people that work for them. Under fascism, Italian business firms were run like military establishments, and until just a few years ago it was quite common for big firms to employ retired military officers to head their personnel departments. Today, relations between superiors and subordinates are a good deal franker and less formal then they were—particularly if the superior has spent some time in the United States. But a Milanese management consultant contends (only half humorously) that "even so, in some companies it is still not enough to tell the boss you agree with his plan—you have to go on and say, 'Boss, I have *always* agreed with your plans.' " In Italian companies there is no pretense that everybody is really equal; in Italy bosses are still bosses. . . .

Before the emergence of the new class of professional managers, Italian businessmen were apt to look on business only as a way to make money for themselves and their families, not as an institution with social responsibilities. Their assumption was that if society happened to benefit by business, it was up to society to be grateful. The older view is apparent in a remark made last year by Franco Marinotti, the seventy-one-year-old head of Snia Viscosa, Italy's biggest producer of synthetic fibers. In answer to a question about Italian politics, Marinotti replied: "I want to work. Just let them leave me alone. If they don't leave me alone I'll go into the country and paint."

The young managers see things quite differently. Strongly democratic in their political sympathies, they believe that private business, at least when it is big business, is justified only if it serves social ends.

> The economic and political future of the country presents quite a remarkable responsibility for the manager [a steel-company executive wrote recently]. He has the burden of erasing the widespread belief that managers . . . are against all progress and change and are worried only about keeping prices high and production low. . . . The manager will bear a heavy responsibility in proving that economic and political freedom can coexist in countries like Italy.

This attitude is widely shared by young executives, and explains why so many of them, while opposing any further nationalization of Italian industry, nevertheless support the government's recent decision to take over the electric-power industry. They support it mainly on the ground that the industry's owners had ignored their obligation to help alleviate, through industrial development, the desperate poverty of most southern Italians.

Furthermore, while admiring the talents of men like Marinotti, who have been largely responsible for the Italian miracle, the young managers question whether these talents will serve Italian business so well in the future. They worry about what will happen when Italian industry no longer enjoys the competitive advantage of labor costs a good deal lower than the general European level, and argue that too much of industry's profits is going into jewels and yachts, and not nearly enough into research. "The base is weak in Italy," an oil-company executive remarks. "I often ask myself: Is this a real boom? Or is it a special situation? Can we Italians only copy, or can we make original things? Can we improve without doing more research?"

Finally, the new professional managers are far more convinced than their predecessors of the need to build bridges, both social and economic, across the abyss that separates poor Italians from the middle classes and the rich. They applaud the housing and swimming pools and running tracks that big companies like Fiat and Montecatini provide for their workers. But they doubt that paternalism alone, however enlightened, will ever make communism go away, and they consider it in any case a poor substitute for industrial relations based on bargaining equality. Such relations now scarcely exist in Italy, where employers and union leaders often seem more interested in wiping each other off the face of the earth than in striking real bargains. The new managers also think business should throw its weight (and money) behind an enormous expansion of Italian schools, and an enormous increase in scholarship aid. Their point is that true democracy will not be achieved in Italy until every child, however poor, has a chance to become a lawyer, or a doctor, or a scientist—or a business executive.

ITALIAN AGRICULTURE [8]

Like other members of the European Common Market, Italy faces a future of challenge in agriculture. It is the challenge of shedding the fetters of nationalism in the interests of broader, "community" agricultural efficiency. And it is an enormous one, since the agricultural economies of most of the European countries have been built up behind highly protective tariff walls and have, therefore, taken on definite and deeply rooted patterns.

Speaking of the objectives of agriculture in the Common Market, or European Economic Community (EEC), Professor Mario Bandini, one of Italy's leading agricultural experts, said that EEC agricultural planners had in mind a situation such as evolved in earlier years in the United States—that is, specialization of crops in various zones where climate and soil conditions are most suitable for their economic production.

Italy, therefore, considered as the natural producer of fruit, vegetables, and rice in the community, ideally would be expected to concentrate on these rather than on other forms of produce.

No wonder there is a certain amount of alarm in Italian agricultural quarters since this more or less cuts across the old-

[8] From "EEC Tests Italian Agriculture," by Walter Lucas, free-lance writer. *The Christian Science Monitor* (Eastern edition). p Cl. My. 7, '63. Reprinted by permission.

established pattern of the Italian agricultural economy. Here wheat has been the backbone of Italian farming, with production swelling to 9.55 million metric tons in 1962, or 2 million more than the average in the four prewar seasons.

Inquiring among experts and practicing farmers about Italian farm matters, two sets of figures follow one around. They are that, while 27 per cent of the nation's labor force is engaged on the land, agriculture produces only 17 per cent of the total national income and that 89 per cent of the total number of farmers, occupying about one third of the available land, are working less than twenty-two acres each (the average being about six acres).

These two sets of figures are in a way related, since this evidence of low earnings from agriculture is partly due to the excessive fragmentation of land which, in turn, precludes modern farming practices.

Correction of this lopsided picture has been the objective of the many costly piecemeal measures taken by the government since the war. It is the objective, too, of the new comprehensive Five-Year Agricultural Development Plan (known as the "Green Plan") which was approved by Parliament in June 1961.

The plan provides for an annual expenditure of about $150 million over a period of five years. Its aim is to boost the quantity and quality of over-all agricultural production and to reduce costs. At the same time it seeks to reorganize the present land-tenure system and create a larger number of viable farming units for a more highly scientific and mechanized system of farming.

Such measures are essential if Italy is to meet the challenge from the more highly organized and productive agricultural systems of some of the other Common Market countries.

There are several factors to be recognized in Italian farming. For instance, there is the nature of the terrain, 20 per cent of which comprises plains and 80 per cent hilly or mountainous country, often unsuitable for mechanization.

Then there is the difference between the north and the south of the country. In the south, which is generally economically depressed, there still is the great population pressure of a poor and often illiterate peasantry on a land which is long on sun and short on water.

Then, apart from tariffs, very often of 50 per cent, there always has been government support for certain types of farming—a support, which, together with the tariffs, may have to be removed when the Common Market comes into full operation in 1970.

The government pays a fixed price for a large percentage of the wheat crop delivered to government granaries. There is similar support for corn, sugar beet, and tobacco, the latter two crops going to the government sugar and tobacco monopoly. Without these supports and the corresponding fixing of market prices, these crops would have to be priced much higher to the public in order for the farmer to make any profit at all.

But despite its still halting progress, there has been a tremendous improvement in Italy's agricultural situation since the war. There also has been a phenomenal drop in the numbers employed on the land—from 49 per cent of the total employed population twenty-five years ago to the present figure of 27 per cent.

This migration from the countryside to the cities and to other European countries has done something to lift the pressure off the land, but it has also had some adverse effects.

Quite often good land near industrial centers has been abandoned. For instance, the rice fields, which are concentrated near Milan, have been drained of labor. This accounts for the 15 per cent decline in the production of rice which is one of Italy's most valuable crops and one which has a future in the Common Market.

Apart from the noticeable increase in wheat production—though most of it is soft wheat and Italy has to import a certain amount of hard wheat to meet its milling needs—the most remarkable development since the war has been in fruit and vegetables.

The deciduous fruit crop increased from an average 860,000 tons in 1936-1939 to 4,460,000 tons in 1962; citrus fruit rose from 706,000 tons to 1,101,000 tons and vegetables, including potatoes, from 3,893,000 to 7,555,000 tons. The biggest individual increases have been in apples, pears, peaches, oranges, and tomatoes.

All this has given the send-off to a new canning and processing industry, which should do something to encourage further expansion of these crops. Certainly Italy is in a position now to meet some of the demands of the Common Market countries and to build up export surpluses outside that area.

The steady improvement in the Italian standard of living has naturally been reflected in agriculture. For one thing it has considerably increased the consumption of meat; this, in turn, has been responsible for the domestic output of livestock and an increase in the production of corn by over a million tons since before the war.

Despite the doubling of beef and pork production, however, Italy still has to import nearly half its meat requirements. According to some experts, it will have to continue doing so for some time to come, especially since, under the Common Market agricultural provisions, France is expected to cater to Italy's and Germany's needs for imported meat.

Much of this improvement in Italy's agricultural production is due to better farming practices and mechanization.

In 1946 Italy was almost entirely a land of the hoe, the scythe, and the ox-drawn plow. In that year there were only 51,950 tractors in use, and in the majority of cases these were in the more highly and intensively cultivated areas of the fertile Po Valley.

Today there are 675,844 mechanized units in use all over Italy, even in the depressed areas of the south.

This rapidly developing use of machines is expected, together with the increase in cooperatives and easy credits for the farmer, to lift Italian agriculture into a more industrialized stage so that it can hold its own in the dawning Common Market era.

SUPERMARKETS HIT ITALY [9]

Effects on Italy's economy of American-style supermarkets are considerable already. Indications are that they have just begun.

For example, the Communists, who objected strongly to Florence's first such supermarket, may not admit it, but it is a known fact that Supermarket Italiani has helped reduce Florence's food costs. Before they were the second highest in the country; today they are a little above average.

How did this happen? It's the age-old story of competition.

[9] From "Supermarkets Dent Italian Food Costs," by Keith de Folo, free-lance writer. *The Christian Science Monitor* (Eastern edition). p 19. Mr. 29, '63. Reprinted by permission.

In a desperate attempt to compete with the supermarket's lower prices, Florentine shopkeepers have narrowed the price gap from 20 per cent above Supermarket Italiani to 15 per cent. By converting to self-service, many stores have reduced costs and improved business.

Since the arrival of the first supermarket, seventy-five modern food shops have sprung up in Florence. By imitating the supermarkets, more merchants have profited than have suffered.

There are always the exceptions. Supermarket Italiani has put five shopkeepers out of business. But even this story doesn't end tragically.

One shopkeeper is now the pastry foreman in the supermarket bakery, another is in charge of a fruit and vegetable department, and the daughters of others work as cashiers. . . .

Florence's new, shiny supermarket at Via Massacio 280 is the eleventh to be opened by IBEC-Italian cooperation since 1957, when the first Supermarket Italini premiered in Milan. (Today, there are six in Milan.)

Nothing describes the success of these supermarkets more eloquently than Milan's nearly sixty American-styled superettes and supermarts which are operated solely by Italians.

Everyone is making a profit, and the Communists haven't said a word. IBEC has scheduled six more supermarkets in Milan during the next two years.

Business is so good in Florence at the five stores (80,000 sales a week) that Supermarket Italiani is going into the drygoods business. Says the Florence manager:

"Profits of soft goods in Italy are highly exaggerated—40 per cent net. We want to shake up this business a little, bring prices down to a realistic level."

The lower floor of the newest store will be converted into a Woolworth-type bargain basement. Sweaters, shirts, socks, dresses, ties, blouses—"anything you can carry out"—will be sold for prices that will make the signoras sing and the Communists groan.

Undoubtedly, Italy's great surge of prosperity during the past fifteen years (rivaled only by [that of] West Germany) is mainly responsible for the success of the supermarkets. Without an amazing recovery from wartime destitution, nothing—not even the cleverest American know-how—could make and save money in Italy.

A scene on the opening day of the newest supermarket points up Italy's postwar phenomenon. A hunched, white-haired lady pushed her buggy through the jammed aisles.

She smiled and joyfully waved her arm over the tins and packages from forty-two countries—pineapple juice from South Africa; cocktail sausages from Denmark; tuna from Japan; caviar from Norway; frozen turkeys from Broadway, Virginia, U.S.A. The great majority of products, however, whether soups, meat, "pasta," or fruits, are tinned and packaged in Italy.

Her buggy was piled high with food as the old lady trundled toward one of the thirteen clicking cash registers. She looked as simple and innocent as any Italian grandmother. Turning to a housewife, she smiled and nodded:

"Signora, I'm certainly glad the Americans won the war. If the Italians had won, we would never have seen anything like this supermarket!"

IV. THE MEZZOGIORNO: THE OTHER ITALY

EDITOR'S INTRODUCTION

The traveler who approaches Italy from the north, crossing the great passes of the Alps into the rich industrial belt that covers the top third of the nation, cannot help being impressed by the striking prosperity of a highly industrialized society. The giant factories of Turin, the sleek wealth and huge skyscrapers of Milan, the well-being that marks Bologna, Reggio Emilia and Genoa—all these are testaments to the dynamism and prosperity of today's Italy. But those travelers who do not penetrate south of Rome are perhaps unaware of another Italy: an Italy where industrialization is barely beginning; where millions of peasants eke out a bare existence on land that does not even belong to them; where the few live in splendor and the many live in misery; where a refrigerator or a telephone is an undreamed-of luxury. This is "the other Italy"—the Italy south of Rome—the "*Mezzogiorno,*" as the Italians call it. This is the land that, until recently, time seems to have forgotten. As the title of Carlo Levi's book on the *Mezzogiorno* says, "Christ stopped at Eboli" —a village near Naples.

But today there is a new feeling of hope in the air. The government has poured billions of lire into a ten-year program to raise the standard of living in the south and to furnish a sound economic base for the future development of the area. Billions have been spent, millions have perhaps been wasted, but changes are already taking place. A fishing village in Sicily is now the site of a giant petrochemical plant, a backwater port in Calabria has become the home of one of the largest and most modern steel mills in Europe.

True, there has been progress, but there must be a great deal more before the two Italies, north and south, become one. The articles in this section deal with the problems of the *Mezzogiorno* and the dramatic changes which are coming.

The first article, by the New York *Times* correspondent C. L. Sulzberger, examines the knitting together of north and south Italy. This is followed by an article in which the Italian writer

Luigi Barzini examines the differences in customs and personality which make it difficult for the two Italies to become one. In the third selection Gabriel Gersh deals with the effect of industrialization and reform on the people of southern Italy, and in the fourth Claire Sterling of *The Reporter* discusses the economic changes taking place in the *Mezzogiorno*. Walter Lucas, in the *Christian Science Monitor*, writes about the government development fund: the Cassa per il Mezzogiorno; and in the final article a correspondent for *The Times* of London gives a first-hand account of the industrialization of the south.

NORTH MEETS SOUTH [1]

Italy's own oldest and most massive problem is the south or *Mezzogiorno*. In *Christ Stopped at Eboli,* one of the many famous books about this area, Carlo Levi wrote that its impoverished inhabitants felt neither like "Christians" nor "human beings" but like "beasts, beasts of burden, or even less than beasts, mere creatures of the wild."

For an Italian, the "south" means everything below Rome, much as for the American it means everything below Washington. The most complex single issue is that of Naples, which somehow includes all that is wrong in the *Mezzogiorno* but also somehow remains apart. Naples is—and looks—a former royal capital which, since it lost this role in 1860, has never forgotten its grandeur.

The city egotistically sees itself thus: "There are inner Neapolitans, outer Neapolitans, those who live near Naples, peasants in the field, Christians and Turks; such is the world."

The first attempt to aid the south was in a 1903 law for the industrialization of Naples. Since then there have been vaster programs culminating in that launched in 1950 as the Cassa per il Mezzogiorno. Its scheduled investments end in 1965, by when it will have spent a total of approximately $2.5 billion.

As a result of this massive scheme, perceptible social changes are occurring. In the old days the southerner was often an illiterate conservative. Today his son is often a literate radical.

[1] From "Italy Starts to Unify at Last," by C. L. Sulzberger, foreign affairs correspondent, New York *Times*. New York *Times*. p 30. Ag. 15, '62. Copyright by The New York *Times*. Reprinted by permission.

Together with schools, hygiene and housing, new ideas are coming in.

Levi said of the south: "Unless there is a peasant revolution we shall never have a true Italian revolution, for the two are identical." Ugo La Malfa, Minister of the Budget, comments: "We have a peasant emigration, not a peasant revolution."

He refers to the exodus of job-seeking southerners to north Italian and Common Market industrial areas. Unemployment here is thus rapidly shrinking. Unfortunately, however, arable land is being abandoned. Together with television aerials and automobiles, evincing higher living standards, one also sees fallow olive orchards and vineyards. For the spreading TV network and the increasing number of letters from those who have left bring an awareness of modern life and the potential of well-being. The southern peasant is no longer content to stay a southern peasant.

A heritage of inefficiency and corruption reduces the value of the Cassa scheme. Some estimate that perhaps 20 per cent of what is being spent is lost. The south used to be called "a cemetery for public works." But the persistence and scale of investment are having a notable effect and the preconditions for modern society are developing.

North Italy, with its humming factories and electric power grids, gradually approaches industrial saturation. Therefore, encouraged by the Cassa's impact, big business is for the first time beginning to move south. Socially this is of enormous significance.

The traveler through this lovely, backward southland can now for the first time see evidence of improvement. In the past the *Mezzogiorno* had been largely ignored by an Italy focusing on dreams of empire. Only since war amputated its final colonies did Rome recognize that the south had indeed always been treated like a colony itself.

This situation has changed and factories, roads, power plants at last are tying this region into the latter twentieth century. Even nostalgic Naples, with its teeming slums and memories of a royal past, is being dragged into the historic present.

The gap between south and north is still immense because the north sucks up increasing wealth from the Common Market. But this gap must soon start to diminish. Today, indeed, there is a prospect that Italy's unification, proclaimed more than a century ago, will soon become a social and economic fact as well as a political expression.

THE TWO ITALIES [2]

Is Italy one, as she appears to be to the casual visitor and as all the books confirm? Or can she be more exactly described as an arbitrary union of two separate countries, "*le due Italie,*" as the Italians say, inhabited by two separate people, as superficially alike but fundamentally dissimilar and antagonistic as, for instance, the Arabs and the Jews?

Italy's case, of course, is not unique. Almost invisible divisions exist in most other countries. In old unified nations like France, Great Britain, or Spain, the people also like to distinguish between their southern and northern types. Such characters are part of the popular lore. They appear on the stage, in the cinema, in proverbs, jokes and tales, often in their regional costumes and always with their traditional traits, as fixed and recognizable as masks from the *Teatro dell' Arte.* Still, they are usually nothing more than relics of the past, unimportant distinctions in the unified national character, with little relation to actual reality. Only rarely, and then only in the most extreme historical emergencies, do people betray their national loyalties and fight for their regional allegiances.

In other countries, however, whose political union was achieved only recently against heavy odds by fortunate minorities and is still fragile, such division between north and south tends to be much more important than mere cracks which are easily papered over. They are seldom matter for jokes. They are the outward signs of a definite cleavage, the cause of deep-seated tensions which make political life insecure, unbalanced, and dangerous. All decisions must be made with the need to keep the country together clearly in mind. Few real problems are soberly assessed and solved. Imaginary problems always have precedence, phony issues on which it is easier to gain the superficial consent of the majority. In such breakable countries politicians usually prefer vast aggressive plans, nationalistic myths, colonial wars, wars against weaker and unprepared neighbors,

[2] From "The Difference in the South," by Lugi Barzini, Italian author. *Encounter.* 18:7-17. Je. '62. Reprinted by permission.

and other such stirring adventures, which allow the people to forget their differences and find an emotional but unstable appearance of unity, rather than dull, long-term, but useful programs.

This necessity also helps to explain the history of Italy in the last hundred years. A peaceful, unmilitary, reasonable, and realistic people dedicated itself to colonial adventures (from the occupation of Massawa in 1885 to the conquest of Libya in 1911 and Ethiopia in 1935), to backbreaking military expenditures (which included the maintenance of an army and a navy among the largest in Europe), and to strenuous and sometimes ludicrous attempts to maintain at all costs the rank of a Great Power. All this necessarily retarded or prevented the development of political institutions, the improvements of the administrative machinery, the training of an elite, the education of the masses, the promotion of industry and commerce, and the modernization of more backward areas.

There were other factors that contributed to the making of Italy what she was and what she is today. Still, the difference between her two halves and the fragility of her national unity were among the more important. They often forced governments of the Right and of the Left to pursue identical projects. Massawa was occupied by the Right-wing, jingoist Prime Minister Francesco Crispi, Tripoli by the Left-wing "*liberale*" Giovanni Giolitti. The ultimate exasperation and consequence of such policies was, in the end, the rise of fascism. Italy's ills helped to determine not only her history but that of Europe and the world. Italy's future welfare and existence as a free and Western nation still largely depend on how well the problem of the coexistence of north and south, the "*problema del Mezzogiorno,*" is understood, studied, and solved. Inevitably one is led to speculate how large an influence Italy's insecurity may again have on the peace of Europe and the rest of the world.

Whole libraries have been filled with studies on the ancient "*problema,*" from the historic investigation by Leopoldo Franchetti and Sidney Sonnino in 1876, down to Danilo Dolci's and Carlo Levi's emotional denunciations. Parliamentary committees, economists, sociologists, historians, scholars, geographers, moralists, politicians, and mere journalists have all attempted to define the reasons why "*le due Italie*" were "*due*" and not "*una,*" and why the gap between them was so difficult to fill. It is, in fact, a magic gap, which appears to grow wider and deeper as more is done to fill it. Why? . . .

All scholars understandably start from a similar presumption, that southerners and northerners are fundamentally the same people but that fortuitous circumstances of one kind or another have temporarily separated them morally, culturally, and economically. They have all been disappointed. No elimination of fortuitous circumstances has yet corrected in the slightest degree the difference between Italians. Few experts have tried to start from what is obvious: the acceptance of the existence of two countries speaking the same language. All the rest necessarily follows, the reasons why the south does not prosper and why all legislation designed to make it prosper hitherto seems to have failed. . . .

There is no doubt that all Italians, observed from a distance, have a family resemblance. They all come from more or less the same stock, have predominantly dark hair, dark eyes, and vivacious expressions. In general they have all experienced similar historical vicissitudes, learned approximately the same lessons through the past centuries, conceived a similar philosophy of life, shared more or less the same hopes and aspirations, and have developed the same talents in order to survive. Italians consider that living is the principal aim of life. They pursue happiness "*all'italiana*," that is they try to further their own private welfare . . . rather than that of society.

They must, therefore, defend themselves and their families against the envy, hatred, ill will, greed, and treachery of the outside world, the state, society, law, and the mighty. They must be prepared to survive natural calamities, historical convulsions, and political upheavals. Unlike the inhabitants of older nations, politically better organized and more advanced, Italians have learned to rely less on collective institutions and organizations and more on their own private virtues and public vices, their personal power, adaptability, charm, intelligence, and shrewdness. In Italy, families often prosper while society decays. The Italian Republic has been defined as a "loose federation of families." . . .

What is this difference [between north and south]?

We have seen that both northerners and southerners want, above all, to protect themselves and their families from risks. They want to survive and see to it that their sons, grandsons, and their progenies survive, defying society, history, cataclysms, and adverse fortune for as long as possible. Here the resemblance stops.

The northerner thinks that there is only one sure way to achieve these aims: the acquisition of wealth, "*la ricchezza.*" Only wealth can assure the family's defense. The southerner, on the other hand, thinks that only power, prestige, and authority will do the job.

The northerner of whatever class is therefore perpetually trying to acquire wealth in its various forms. He wants a job, a good job, a better job. He wants land, capital, credits, shares, houses, technical and scientific knowledge which can be converted into high salaries, executive posts in good businesses, expensive and rare university degrees, which assure him better-paid employment, and will undergo any sacrifice in order to gain these advantages for himself or his sons. He wants a rich wife, rich daughters and sons-in-law, and rich friends. He is very close to being a pure *homo economicus.*

The southerner, on the other hand, wants to be obeyed, admired, respected, feared, and envied. For him the important aims in life are rank, influence, power in any one of its many forms, not wealth but the appearance of wealth. In whatever rank of society he is born, he will pursue those aims. The little peasant, as well as the landed proprietor, will cultivate the gratitude of powerful friends and relatives, the fear of his enemies, and the respect of everybody. . . .

The northerner who seems to pursue power only does so because power will generate more wealth, and the southerner who wants to accumulate money regards this merely as another way of achieving a higher and more respected place in society. There are, for instance, northern politicians in Rome who use their dominating position in order to amass a fortune. There are, likewise, southerners who amass fortunes in order to become deputies, under-secretaries, and cabinet ministers. Generally speaking, southerners tend to make money in order to rule, northerners to rule in order to make money.

Still, the difference, while not always identifiable in individuals, is always discernible in the two societies. It permeates every detail. It strengthens the contrasting characteristics of the two sections. It widens the gap. Official Italy has apparently succeeded merely in unifying names, labels and titles, but not reality.

Take a "*prefetto*," for instance. He is a functionary appointed by the central government, who rules over a province. He is always a southerner. Only southerners, as we have seen, like badly-paid jobs with honorific titles and high protocol precedence. He rates the title of "*Eccelenza*," like a Roman prince, and sits very high at any table.

Nothing would be more misleading than to think that the "*prefetto*" in a northern province has any resemblance to his colleague in a southern province. In the north he is an inconspicuous bureaucrat. Nobody remembers his name. He is seldom invited except to official functions. In the south he is ruler, *ras*, chieftain, *catapan*, a social leader. He is surrounded by courtiers and sycophants. He goes to banquets, weddings, funerals, and christenings. His word, a mere suggestion on the telephone, or a wish whispered as to himself, is law. He sometimes can still (and always could in the past) swing elections. When he goes by, people bow low and take their hats off.

It is pointless to pass judgment on either of these two societies, to say which is better, more civilized or advanced, which is more likely in the long run to provide the "greatest good for the greatest number." Is the northerner really happier than the southerner? He has considerable material advantages. Do they compensate for the spiritual poverty, the leveling, the crude hedonism, the infantile culture, and the harsh discipline which are inseparable from an advanced industrialized society? Is the southerner happier, then? He lives a poorer but freer life. He is not bound by rigid schedules. He defends himself, like the red Indians in the prairies, and enjoys using all his faculties in the daily struggle to overwhelm his competitors. He has time to pursue idle and wasteful passions. His life is nearer nature and natural instincts. Do these advantages compensate for the poverty and insecurity of his life?

Consider what great benefits southerners contributed to past Italian achievements. A people wholly dedicated to the rational and scientific pursuit of wealth inevitably becomes dull. Civilization and the graces of life flourish best where there are disinterested, dedicated, and intelligent people, men who accept a lower standard of living for the sake of more satisfying occupations and who prefer dignity, fame, authority, or ease of conscience to money or security: scholars, poets, artists, novelists, saints, philosophers, jurists, eccentrics, spendthrift aristocrats, *et al.* The *Mezzogiorno* has produced a great majority of such characters in Italian life. Italy's debt to them is great.

The state has been cheaply run for decades, up to the last war, by able and honest southern bureaucrats. The universities were and are staffed mainly by southern professors. Some of the best novels in contemporary Italy were written by southerners, the Sicilians Verga, Capuana, De Roberto, Brancati. Vittorini, and now Giuseppe Tomasi di Lampedusa. Her greatest playwright, Pirandello, was born in Agrigento. Her greatest philosopher, Croce, and one of her greatest poets, d'Annunzio, were born in the Abruzzi. Her colonies were administered with great personal sacrifice by competent officials from the south. Most of the staff officers in the army and navy were from the southern half. The Sicilians formed a nucleus of the Foreign Service where they excelled because their native qualities were the same as those which are indispensable in the conduct of foreign negotiations. Most heroes in her wars were from the south. The principal publishing houses entirely dedicated to unprofitable culture were in Bari (Laterza), Naples (Ricciardi), and Messina (Principato). They kept the Italian soul alive in the dark times of the Fascist dictatorship, as the Benedictines did in the remote Middle Ages. . . .

The fact that many southern traits and habits may be classified as typical of an "agrarian," "feudal," or "pre-capitalistic" society is only a partial but a misleading explanation. It again presupposes that southerners would be northerners if only they were given the chance. There is no doubt that in the *Mezzogiorno* one still encounters beliefs and habits belonging to earlier ages. One often finds, for instance, to quote a few obvious examples, love of display and pomp, jealous defense of one's own personal honor, contempt for productive occupations, disdain for trade, and disregard for the careful administration of one's own property. One finds the fierce loyalties of the humble for the mighty, and the complementary feelings of the mighty, who must lead, protect, and care for their "*clientes*" in all circumstances. One also finds that southerners prefer their own private laws to recourse to the official machinery, the police and the courts. It is admittedly true that all these were common traits in Europe before the industrial revolution a few centuries ago.

The point is not that such habits survived, but why they survived at all. Southerners, when deploring the vices and virtues of their people, call them "*spagnolismi,*" or remnants of the Spanish domination. The Spanish dominated Milan for about as long as they dominated the Kingdom of Naples; they also dominated Flanders and the Low Countries for centuries. Why is it that only in the *Mezzogiorno* were their teachings adopted apparently forever while they were easily forgotten elsewhere? Why should the Milanese, the Belgians, the Dutch have developed the un-Spanish virtue of business enterprise, industry, and the appreciation of the value of money which southerners never learned?

Why did the Neapolitans and the Sicilians cling to "feudal" manners, if not because their own national character made them more adaptable to such a way of life? The industrial revolution started in the north of Italy at about the same time as in the south. Factories sprang up in both regions within a few years of each other. Why were they promoted by the king in the south and by private individuals in the north? Why did they decay rapidly in the south, after the unification of the country, and flourish in the north?

The point which interests us here is simply that southerners learned from all foreigners, including the Spaniards, only that which suited them, and always clung to their own way of life through thick and thin, in spite of everything, sometimes daring defeat, poverty, degradation, and desperation in order not to betray their own nature and habits. Like the Chinese, they digested and assimilated foreign rulers, ways, and ideas, and accepted them only when transformed into something of their own. They could never be untrue to themselves. Just as a weak people does, when invaded and dominated by powerful foreigners, they often produced in the past and still produce today comical and unconscious parodies of the north. The two French kings of Naples at the time of Napoleon's rule over Europe, Joseph Bonaparte and Joachim Murat, introduced the Code Napoléon into the southern legal system. It was a revolutionary initiative. After a few years, the new laws were modified, interpreted, and applied in such a way that the French lawyers could not recognize them. Or take the railways. When the tracks were laid in the north, they followed the shortest and cheapest routes between cities. In the south, they meandered all over the landscape, in order to pass in front of obscure hamlets where some powerful person or his friend was born, or to lengthen the mileage and enrich the contractor responsible for the construction of some particular section.

The southerners' attachment to their own ways is often concealed. It is not now fashionable to praise what are officially considered to be reactionary prejudices and vices. Confronted with the modern world and its complicated requirements, southerners react with insincere praise, sincere envy, and polite cynicism. . . .

Some of these disillusioned southerners have turned for salvation to the Communist party, to a system which appears even more hostile to their way of life than the north is. Efficient, disciplined, egalitarian, "scientific," the Communist creed makes northern Italy and industrialized Europe seem almost lackadaisical and benign by comparison. What southerners like in the Communist party is its hatred for the bourgeois and liberal revolution, its hope for a new hierarchical world, almost feudal in its stratified construction, where free competition is abolished, and any man with powerful friends can defend his position in life.

Southerners naturally cannot go back to the happy days of Ferdinand II, the king who spoke dialect and knew his people's foibles. He used to say: "My kingdom is an island, protected by salt water on three sides and holy water on the fourth." The Papal States no longer defend the northern border from the rest of Europe. At the same time, southerners have little liking for and understanding of the modern world, in which they do not feel at ease, are often beaten and humiliated by duller competitors, who ignore the fine points of the art of living but stick diligently to their chores. Southerners, as we have seen, cannot easily or quickly change themselves. They can only sometimes make believe they do. Their malaise has no apparent cure. They cannot become efficient northerners, bent merely on making money. Yet they cannot endure their condition of "inferior," or "backward" people.

This is the psychological heart of the *"problema del Mezzogiorno."*

The *problema* is nothing new. It goes back to the early nineteenth century, when northern "patriots" and "liberals" wanted to join the rest of Italy in a unified state also in order to dump their unsolvable problems into the common lap, and let northerners take care of them. After the unification, the south immediately started clamoring for special attention. Cavour's dying words, a few months after the proclamation of the new kingdom, were dedicated to *"i poveri napoletani."*

Special laws, special projects, special programs of public works, special credits for business ventures, special appropriations for the south have been a constant feature of Italian policy since the beginning of the century. Giovanni Giolitti and Benito Mussolini dedicated some of the best years of their lives to satisfying the south's claims for particular attention. Since 1950 the new democratic republic has spent in the south more than double the sum which had been spent in the previous half century. The progress has been immense. Nevertheless, the old ills are still present. . . .

Because of . . . [his] ancient obsession with power and the visible outward marks of power—authority, rank, prestige—the southerner is a sharper political animal than the northerner. He can weigh up at a glance the true resolution and the resources of an opponent. He knows when that resolution and those resources exceed his own and the exact moment when his own fear is smaller than his opponent's. This political flair he has had to develop since infancy, so as to get the simplest things done in the world. Every southerner, from the land-owning princes to the illiterate herdsmen and day laborers, has been brought up to obey privately the rules which in more advanced countries are valid only in public affairs, political struggles, international negotiations, and the great issues of war and peace. He naturally negotiates only from strong positions; he divides, whenever he can, his opponents in order to rule over them; he "licks them or joins them" like every true statesman.

Naturally enough, southerners who easily conquered all-powerful but badly-paid positions in the Italian state administration and in politics, exerted an immense influence in the shaping of the policy for the solution of the problem of their native land.

The majority of cabinet ministers, under-secretaries, high officials, technicians, managers of state enterprises, state banks, and employees who were of southern extraction, did all they could to help. In the last sixty years practically everything that government intervention, state money, and politics could do was done.

A short journey through any part of southern Italy by rail or car will reveal this.

The visitor will see everywhere a large amount of buildings erected with public money in the last two or three centuries, more than in any other country, all of which are in various stages of preservation. He will first see (chronologically speaking) the Cyclopean structures of his great-grandfather's time, erected by the first Bourbons, Joseph Bonaparte, and Joachim Murat, and finally the incredible amount of works done in the first fifteen years of Ferdinand II's reign. This still constitutes the great foundation, the majority of basic works: roads, bridges, harbors, public buildings, churches, and hospitals. Then, the more familiar and modest buildings of the early Victor Emmanuel III period, the years before the First World War, followed by the more numerous, lavish, splendid, and rhetorical attempts of Mussolini to perpetuate his name and the fame of his regime. Lastly, the glittering new buildings erected by his contemporaries.

In each of the older architectural epochs, note the execrable state of repair. In the suburbs of Naples, for instance, some factories were built only at the beginning of the century but are now falling down. The plaster is peeling from the walls. It is impossible to read the name of the firm painted on the façade, decades ago, obliterated by the sun and the dust. Rotten roof beams bend under the weight of moss-encrusted tiles. Doors hang from rusty hinges. The courtyards are piled with refuse, dilapidated machinery, weather-beaten packing cases, and litter which nobody carries away amongst the wild grass. The factories still run, of course. Somehow, on the brink of collapse, the wheels turn. The reason is that economic criteria are considered secondary in the south. The factory is not a strictly economic enterprise. It was built with public money grants and special tax facilities. It is not meant to function efficiently. Its shoddy products are probably cheap enough to sell in the market, but cheap only because interest is low, no money is spent for modernization, upkeep, renovation, and wages are lower than elsewhere, miserably low, in fact. . . .

The lack of upkeep strikes one everywhere. Even today, the law enabling the Cassa per il Mezzogiorno to spend millions of lire for the modernization of the country contains no provision whatever for the maintenance of existing works. Maintenance is not considered important in the south because the primary function of any structure is psychological. Factories are not built to produce goods efficiently and cheaply nor to compete with northern enterprises. They are built to be inaugurated with great pomp on the first day, to be admired as a sign of modernity and industrialization, a proof of power, to provoke envy in neighboring villages, to gain the people's gratitude towards the local political patron or the predominating party, and finally to afford a miserable living to a few workers. In the past, when our fathers discovered what eventually happened to public works carried out in the south, they called it "the cemetery of public works." It is still often called that today. . . .

Undoubtedly many things have changed in the south, many more perhaps than the reader of these pages has been led to believe. It is, after all, no longer Ferdinand II's "island." It is part of a contemporary modern nation, part of Europe, part of the contemporary world. It was not sheltered from history. It could not be protected from the influx of world-wide trends. The large amounts of money spent in the last few years could not help having an influence. . . . Emigration to North and South America and to the rest of Europe provoked a return flow of money, new ideas, new habits, and restlessness. For a century and a half able men from the middle class emigrated to central and northern Italy, where they and their descendants now occupy leading positions. (It is only known by few, for instance, that the Pirelli family, founders and owners of a vast rubber empire, are from Taranto.) Southern soldiers brought back northern wives. The movies and television forced the inhabitants of obscure villages to gaze upon an idealized, bourgeois, and well-fed image of the outside world. The sudden and vigorous upsurge of economic activities in the north of Italy after the last war could not help having a weaker but distinct aftereffect on southern life. Unemployed workers go north by the tens of thousands, where they find jobs. Those who are left behind have steadier employment and higher wages.

All this and numerous other factors inevitably changed the appearance, the habits, the life, the ideals of many southerners.

Factories are visible everywhere, new factories, built in the last few years. Some, of course, are already shut. They were built with no clear ideas, not enough money, no experience, to satisfy the usual emotional cravings. Others function. They sometimes produce something which has been manufactured for a long time better and cheaper in the north. The south believes not in specialization (everything that is traditional is thought to bestow less prestige and honor) but in emulation. A few plants, here and there, flourish. They are the factories which nature decreed should be built on the spot because of objective reasons, the vicinity of raw materials, the cheap labor supply, abundant energy, easy transport facilities, etc. Some of them were built by northern firms, taking full advantage of the legislation facilitating economic enterprises in the south. . . .

New quarters in the decrepit cities everywhere look like provincial Brasilias. The very audacity of the architecture denounces, as it does in South America, the fear of appearing old-fashioned, of seeeming anchored to ancient habits, left behind by the march of Progress. The faces of people have changed in the cities and the most prosperous towns. The women are freer and better dressed. The crowds in the streets look better fed. The younger people especially are determined not to eke out a living as their ancestors have always done, no longer to resign themselves to the will of God, the favor of the mighty, the caprice of fortune, and the everlasting *"miseria."* They are taller and straighter than their fathers.

Yet, in spite of all these considerable and sometimes incredible improvements, some of them the result of the will of man and many of circumstances, it would be dishonest to say that the *problema del Mezzogiorno* is on its way to a solution. To begin with, the immense poverty still exists. The presence of its pressure underlies everything. Most of the improvements and modernizations can be observed around a few cities, in some of the most fertile agrarian sections, or in isolated spots specially favored by nature. Everywhere else, where the casual visitor from the north does not usually go, around the corner from a prosperous scene, a stone's throw from the resplendent new hotels, factories, or workers' houses, and almost everywhere in the countryside, the *miseria* is still supreme.

It is a better *miseria,* often comforted by new, modern conveniences, a road, a public telephone, sometimes an aqueduct, sewers, a doctor twice a week, a *miseria* tempered perhaps by the distribution of American surplus flour, condensed milk, and beans to the destitute, but *miseria* nevertheless. Even if, however, the process of modernization should continue, and everything everywhere showed the mark of a definite improvement, if everybody had a roof over his head, enough to eat, a job, relative security, medical care, and an elementary education, the *problema* would still not be solved. The malaise and the restlessness, the feeling of being the victims of historical injustice and the prey of other people's greed, the desire to revolt and break away from united Italy would continue to make political life insecure and Italian unity as fragile as it has always been.

Why? The southerners of course want to live better, to live at the minimum standard of Europeans, to solve some of their most urgent problems. They want all this but they especially want something else. They want to see the gap between north and south disappear. They want to live as well as northerners. Anything else is not acceptable. Anything else is dishonorable. They do not understand why their countrymen should have such splendid living conditions, such wonderful factories, such awe-inspiring hospitals, and so much money, and why such things should be less impressive in the south. Southerners will never be placated until the difference is erased. . . .

As long as the south does not really want prosperity, but moral equality with the north, it spends its efforts and money, as it has always done, not on strictly economic aims but on the display of newly acquired, or not yet acquired, power and prestige. The factories being built are sometimes not factories but monuments to the god Progress or to the goddess Industrialization, visible demonstrations that the city or region is to be considered no longer backward but one of the richest, most modern, and progressive in the world.

It is not surprising, therefore, that such investments do not produce strictly economic results. The *Mezzogiorno* is not getting rich as fast as it could, with the money dedicated to it. What is surprising and disappointing is that the psychological effects on which southerners prefer to lavish their own and other people's money were not fully achieved either. What is surprising and disappointing is the discovery, which is being gradually made, that only investments dictated by strictly northern criteria can, in the long run, produce stable psychological, moral, and political results, and one day really solve the *problema del Mezzogiorno.*

ITALY'S HAUNTED SOUTH [3]

In the spring of 1960 the Piazza Garibaldi, the vast square in front of the main railroad station at Naples, was a temporary desert, man-made to make way for the new station even then rising from the dust as a challenge to the modern grace of rival Rome's famous terminal. Why not an equally worthy station for Naples, the Neapolitans insisted, to receive visitors to this former capital of the southern Italian kingdom, seat of its own kings until Garibaldi came a century ago to make it part of a united Italy? . . .

To many southerners, the intense planning, the open-handedness, the tenacity of purpose, and the feeling of national pride displayed by the government in its feverish preparations for the Olympics, constituted precisely those elements of urgency characteristically lacking in its handling of the enduring problems of the south.

The official celebrations that were held after the 1960 Olympics to mark the centenary of the end of Bourbon rule in Italy belied the grim political and economic realities facing the country today. "Do not be misled by celebrations or claims of national unity," was the warning sounded in 1960. It is still heard frequently today, for north and south are essentially foreign to each other and are united in name more than in reality.

Climate, geography, and history have combined to make the lives of the southerners difficult. Because of constant neglect in the past, the task of coaxing a living from this largely barren terrain is rewarded only with the utmost privation. Most of the south is mountainous, and only the coastal area around Naples, the strip along the Adriatic below Mount Gargano, and the

[3] From article by Gabriel Gersh. *The Progressive.* 27:25-8. Ag. '63. Reprinted by permission.

Tyrrhenian coast of Calabria posses fertile soil capable of producing olives, grapes, and oranges.

Many of the peasants in southern Italy still live in hill towns, originally built for protection against disease, pirates, and invaders, or in villages in the plains, where they till the soil on plots often many miles away from their homes. Vast stretches of treeless plains in Sicily are covered with scrub or wheat—one seventh of Italy's wheat-growing area is in this historic granary—but the yield is hardly more than half the Italian average and less than one third that of Lombardy. One of the causes of this low wheat yield is the shortage of water, which not only prevents the peasants from intensively tilling the soil, but also from living near the land they till.

The major feature of southern Italy's agriculture is still the vast estates (latifundia) owned by absentee landlords. Under Italy's land reform program, poor land from certain large estates has been irrigated and divided into small holdings, each with a small farmhouse. Despite these reforms many peasants still prefer to live in their own hovels and trudge, or ride by mule or scooter, to their patch of land, rather than live on the new but solitary farms. They do not easily adapt to peasant cooperatives which would help them manage their holdings more efficiently.

Whether the land reform program has had an impact on the south cannot yet be judged. Elsewhere in Europe land reform means something different—the accumulation of small holdings into larger ones, so that the best use can be made of mechanization. This is another indication of how retarded is reform in southern Italy. It will be for the next generation to go farther, but the natural rate of population increase may by then have made the small farm quite useless unless many peasants either find another way of earning a living or migrate in even greater numbers to the north.

The south today is beginning to display many hopeful signs, from electric generators to elegant, emancipated girls, but it still remains an astonishingly backward place, a place of mules and ignorant priests, of ancient folkways and taboos, of dust, dirt, distrust, and decadence. It is a place riddled with politics, as one can see from myriad posters plastered on village walls—manifestoes versus declamations, denunciations against denials, clerical black opposing revolutionary red. Some towns of the south greet one with movies and gaudy espresso bars. Others remain so barren and vacuous, emanating such an arid sense of rancor and boredom, that when one arrives in their listless squares, searching for accommodations, or a meal, or a lively face, he is reminded of the nightmarish villages of the Egyptian delta.

The great dream of the impoverished south is the development of industry. Southerners with a knowledge of their history of the past century know that the Neapolitan kingdom saw the first railroad in Italy, the first steamboat, and one of the first steel mills. Although the south, in its own way, was in the forefront of Italian industrialization, it never acquired the solid base necessary for sustained industrial development. That fell an immediate victim to political unification under the northern House of Savoy in 1861, when Italy's industry became based in the northern triangle formed by Milan, Genoa, and Turin. Now, the southerner is aware that his dream of industrialization is realizable only through national government aid on a massive scale.

Monarchist or republican, the cry for government help for the south varies only in particulars. To the people of a hilltop town, set back from the Ionian coast of Calabria, government aid means a new road linking their town with the outside world. To a small town in Lucania it means a cement factory dreamed about for years. To a Sicilian peasant outside Marsala, who is unhappily housed without water on a small plot allotted him under the land reform, it means the digging of a well ("Am I supposed to dig it myself?"). To another southerner it means more schools to overcome illiteracy and provide skilled training.

Government aid means, too, the resurrection of ancient port cities like Crotone, a Calabrian coastal town, which the local authorities point out was in ancient times a prosperous Greek colony and a commercial and cultural center. A Doric column attests to its former glory, to say nothing of the memory of Pythagoras.

The hope of resurrection typified by Crotone is strong elsewhere around the Mediterranean. Africa is awakening and northern Italy has already reached its full stride. Only southern Italy, lamented a Communist school teacher in a small southern village, continues to slumber. The vision of a substantial role for southern Italy in a Mediterranean recharged by an African revival is part of the argument which leading members of the Sicilian Regional Government make to back their assertion that within ten years their island will be one of the most industrialized regions of Italy. It is a belief strongly held in ports such as Naples and Bari which knew greater prosperity during the days of the Fascist empire and can now conceive of improvement from renewed links with Africa.

Is this just a dream? Since 1956, when Egypt's President Gamal Abdel Nasser was making his own contribution to the awakening of the northern stretches of Africa, traffic in the Adriatic port of Bari has decreased each year, even though it is the site of the Levant Fair, an exposition for the entire eastern Mediterranean. On the other hand, the port of Gela, on the south coast, is already the Italian point of entry for oil from North Africa and the Middle East, and the decision to build a bridge over the Straits of Messina between Sicily and the Italian mainland has heartened those Sicilians who envision their island as a highway for trade between Africa and Europe.

One is told in the south that under Mussolini some southerners went happily to fight for an empire in Africa and against the Communists in Spain; now the empire is gone and the Communists are the second largest party in Italy. A century ago southerners fought for Garibaldi while a few took up banditry to harry the newly forged unity. And today? The degree of frustration is reflected in a slogan on the walls of a Lucanian town: "We are Italians, too."

Is the south's claim of neglect by the national government unfair? In some ways it is, because much of the government's effort has not been wasted. Many southerners will admit that conditions have improved, that progress has been made even if it is disappointingly slow, disjointed, and mainly limited to certain areas. But the harsh and inescapable truth is that the government in its first twelve years of concentrated activity in the south has hardly begun to overcome the failures of the one hundred years since the southern kingdom's incorporation into Italy.

Various reports on the government's recent years of activity in the south show that a policy of investment, financial incentives, and public works at best has only prevented the gap between northern and southern living standards from widening as much as it might if nothing were done. For instance, recent statistics disclosed that from 1951 to 1962 the difference between the per capita income in the south and the rest of the country widened by 1.3 per cent. Even more discouraging is the fact that in the last twelve years the contribution of the south to total national income has fallen steadily from 23.5 per cent to 20.3 per cent.

Most startling is the contrast between the dollar value of per capita incomes of the two regions during the same period. While the annual per capita income in the south rose from approximately $200 to $302, in the north it increased from approximately $378 to $685. These figures are disappointing, especially since total investment in the south has been $3.5 billion in the past dozen years. Of this sum, about $1.8 billion has been spent for social-economic overhead—basic transportation and power facilities, $1.6 billion for industrial development, and the rest for schools and educational projects.

Despite the pessimistic implications of these statistics, 1962 produced the first signs that industrialization was beginning to take hold in the south, with Taranto, Latina, and Brindisi as the focal points for private and public investment.

Yet the problems are enormous. A typical example of the south's suffocating economic stagnation is Palma di Montechiaro in western Sicily, where the peasants live with their animals in hovels unfit for human habitation. Famous as the background of Giuseppe di Lampedusa's novel, *The Leopard,* Palma is pervaded by what the author called "the sense of death which even the frantic Sicilian light can never dispel." The town's 20,000 population comprises laborers and peasants who manage to find work only four months a year, earning at most $16 a month. They supplement their meager wages by renting their mules and selling manure.

In several of the larger towns in the south the public works projects have given jobs to many of the jobless. Traveling through these towns, one cannot help being struck by the scale of public building. However, serious problems arise when a particular project is finished. For some months the unemployed have something to do—making a road, building a block of apartments, digging a reservoir. When the work is completed they relapse, more cynical and disgruntled than ever, into unwilling idleness. Many do not understand that such public projects bring returns in the long run; instead, they resign themselves once more to poverty, convinced that, after an abortive gesture by the authorities, nothing has changed.

Because of these factors, the north, with its wealth and dynamism, faces an urgent challenge in the south. It needs to find ways of transforming the south, of enlisting the energies of its people, of seeking new outlets for investment. However, the north's response to this challenge has not been enthusiastic. The northern industrialist, who prefers to expand his factories in the north rather open new ones in the south, argues that available labor in the south, plentiful though it may be, is still unskilled and backward. He also points to the lack of transportation, especially needed to ship raw materials to the south where they are in short supply. The study of the Olivetti factory near Naples, which was the subject of Ottiero Ottieri's moving sociological novel, *Men at the Gate,* has shown that southerners, once given the chance, have the same aptitude for skilled labor as those in the north. A more ominous possibility, however, is that even if industry should come to the south on a large scale, it might already be too late to have the hoped-for effect of a universal provider, for now the trend is to employ fewer men and more machines.

Given the unemployment, poverty, and backwardness of the south, it is hardly surprising that the Communists have made inroads among the workers and peasants. For some time now the Communists have been increasing their efforts in the south.

Many southerners believe that a large number of reforms initiated by the government were attributable to the fear of the dominant Christian Democratic party that inaction would lead to Communist political successes. The Christian Democrats also suffer from the disadvantage of close identification with the landlords and industrialists, and the public awareness of their party's long history of neglect of the south.

The outcome of the recent election in Italy has underlined the anxiety of many Italians for the future of the south. The increase in the Communist vote was registered in every one of the nineteen Italian regions, but it was generally higher in the south than in the north. This was contrary to the expectations of the Communist party, which had feared the loss of many active members who had migrated to the north.

The Communists were able to exploit the grievances, real and imaginary, of the people, and promised them more than the government offered. Moreover, in this election the Communists were helped by two elements whose effectiveness have not yet been accurately gauged—television and the new attitude of the Catholic Church towards politics. Every village in the south has a television-equipped coffee bar in the piazza, where the population gathers in the evening. During the recent election campaign, millions of southerners saw the election dramatized on television by Premier Amintore Fanfani, Communist leader Palmiro Togliatti, and others. Because of their superior television team and the colorful personality of Togliatti, the Communists were able to project a dynamic image to audiences all over Italy.

The second new element was the Vatican's disengagement from politics. Parish priests were no longer bound by instructions to invoke the sanctions of the Church against those who voted for the Left. This loosening of the Church's grip on the voters aided the Communists, for it freed many Italians to cast their votes as their political inclinations, rather than as their consciences, dictated. Togliatti took advantage of this new Church attitude by proclaiming that communism and Catholicism were not incompatible and that Communists and Catholics can work together in harmony for the good of the country.

The effects of these new factors in the last election are difficult to evaluate with any accuracy although they undoubtedly contributed to the gains of the Communists in the south and elsewhere. The election has underscored the failure of Christian Democracy to win the support of the masses in the south. Christian Democracy cannot pose as the popular successor to Bourbon rule in a land steeped in historical tradition. It can claim little kinship with Garibaldi, for he was an anticlerical, still deprecated by the Church authorities who are the party's mentors. Nor can Christian Democracy serve as a renewing force born of antifascism because in most of the south the Allied forces arrived relatively early in World War II, and there was no prolonged heroic role for the Resistance movement in the area.

Inevitably, the main stimulus of Christian Democracy begins and ends in anticommunism. The protagonist and the antagonist in Italian politics, even more in the south than elsewhere, seem to be necessary to each other. This struggle dominates affairs beyond the limits of politics and national elections and casts a shadow of distrust and suspicion over the region.

"There was a life once at this promontory," wrote Norman Douglas, the greatest of English travel writers on southern Italy, from a Calabrian cape. "Argosies touched here, leaving priceless gifts; fountains flowed, and cornfields waved in the genial sun. Doubtless there will be life again; earth and sea are only waiting for the enchanter's wand." Nearly half a century since those words were written, southern Italy still slumbers; the earth and sea are still awaiting the enchanter.

SOUTH OF ROME [4]

[In 1950] the Italian government set out to reclaim the land and people of its economically depressed southern provinces. At the outset the problems seemed appalling, the prospects limited, and the expense—an estimated $2 billion—a heavy burden for a country that was poor itself in those days. Nevertheless, the work has gone on; and while the problems are still appalling and the expense has greatly increased—$12 billion spent so far—the prospects have improved. The south hasn't caught up with the industrial north; it probably is further than ever behind that prosperous region. But it is richer today than all Italy was in 1950, and it has at least an even chance now of achieving a viable economy by 1970.

To anyone familiar with the great derelict lands lying south of Rome, the change in barely a dozen years is stunning. In 1950, southern Italy was still pretty much what a millennium of negligent absentee rule had made it: a ruin of lunar hills and ravaged valleys, with few roads, fewer dams and bridges, very little water, no industry to speak of, a population sunk in torpor, and a soil so exhausted that the peasants' only escape from misery was emigration. Today, the roads have become passable, and the lunar landscape is relieved by thick belts of green—sapling pines, orchards, vegetable beds, luxuriant grapevines under hothouse glass. Instead of leaving Italy, today's migrants move to new jobs in the north. Throughout Apulia, Lucania, and Calabria,

[4] From "Transformation South of Rome," by Claire Sterling, Mediterranean correspondent, *The Reporter*. *The Reporter*. 27:32-4. S. 27, '62. Copyright 1962 by the Reporter Magazine Company. Reprinted by permission.

the most wretched hilltop villages have acquired drinking water, sewers, and electric lights, while some of the larger towns and cities are barely recognizable.

In Matera, the notorious Sassi (cave dwellings) are about to be declared a national monument: their twenty-two thousand former residents have moved into ugly but hygienic modern apartments. In the Lucanian village of Policoro, the peasants who once tilled Baron Giulio Berlingieri's 57,000 acres and slept in his stalls now own his land and live in four-room cottages with bathrooms, refrigerators, television sets, and occasionally a Vespa or ramshackle Fiat to replace the family donkey; many work in the new automated sugar mills and canning factories just down the macadam highway; and the local population has grown from four hundred to ten thousand. In Bari, the waterfront is lined with derricks to prepare the foundations for an industrial zone that will soon turn out trailers, rolling stock, tires, shoes, canned goods, and plastics, while an immense housing project rears up out of the olive groves beyond. In the nearby port of Brindisi, a new petrochemical plant is spreading over an area twice the city's size, and the southernmost port of Taranto is ringed with the elements of a steel-making complex that will be the biggest of its kind in Europe.

While this growth may be striking, it is uneven and is far from adequate for the needs of the region. Even now, the south's 19 million people, well over a third of the national population, account for only a fourth of Italy's consumption and a fifth of the production; its agricultural yield is 40 per cent lower than the north's (which has three times the south's ratio of tractors); and its average annual income is only $450—a lot better than in Spain or Portugal, but only half the north's $900. Furthermore, where the southerner's income has doubled in the last ten years, the northern increase has been 120 per cent. Lately, however, a more encouraging statistic has been registered. . . . [In 1961] the south's income rose faster than the north's (13.6 per cent compared to 8.9 per cent). This is the first sign that the south is beginning to reap the dividends of the prodigious government investment.

Economists have felt all along that there wasn't much use in trying merely to make the individual southerner's life temporarily more bearable. Partial remedies have been applied time and again, only to end in a relapse. The only lasting cure, they have argued, would be to lift the entire region up to something approaching the national levels of production and purchasing power, making it a self-supporting part of the economy rather than a permanent ward of the state. No government has had the means to do that in the past, including the late Alcide de Gasperi's. In 1950 he saw the need and initiated the first postwar development plan. Though his resources were limited, he gave land and credit to peasants on the verge of revolution; built the most urgently needed roads, dams, hospitals, houses, and schools; and developed local handcrafts and tourism. Then the northern miracle happened. Capital became more plentiful, the Common Market came into being, and the south emerged so quickly from its traditional languor that a more ambitious plan became not only desirable and possible, but imperative.

Naturally, a good deal of the old southern mentality remains. But where government agencies continue to meet occasional passive resistance, they also encounter leaders and communities keenly responsive to their plans. Their ablest administrators and technicians today are local men; scores of producing and marketing cooperatives are run by peasant members; and two thirds of the region's new industries have been promoted and are now directed by southerners. Where the peasants once snatched their children from the third grade to work in the fields, they now are eager for more education: there has been such a rush to Lucania's high schools that doctors, lawyers, and engineers are pitching in as volunteer teachers. Above all, where the same peasants were resigned to a lifetime of drudgery, today they have acquired a taste for the fruits of the machine age. No longer are their dreams fulfilled when the title to two stony acres is placed in their hands. In the quest for more money, ease, leisure, and amusement, they are moving from the mountains to the plains, from hamlets to villages, from there to the towns, and then on to the cities, the provincial capitals, the north, and other countries of Western Europe. The problem is no longer how to satisfy their timeless craving for land but how to keep them on it.

Emigration has always been a useful outlet for the south, and the last thing the government wants at the moment is to stop it. If it weren't for cheap southern labor, the northern miracle could not have happened and could not last. Nevertheless, those who go are the cream of southern youth, leaving behind the old and infirm, the women, and those too lacking in enterprise to follow. In losing them, the south loses not only all the money it took to raise them—an estimated $3 billion for the 2 million who have emigrated in the last decade, half of them to the north—but all it has cost to coax fertility into the farms they are abandoning. Up to a point, this constant outward flow is helpful and even necessary, since it reduces the number of mouths that each southern acre must feed. But beyond that point, it could drain away the forces indispensable to a rational system of agriculture and industry, excluding the south from the Common Market's lucrative profits, and withdrawing it from the race to draw abreast of the twentieth century. With 380,000 southern workers going north in 1961 alone, the situation is serious already. If the northern boom continues, the south may have no more than two or three years to catch up with the rest of the country or face the failure of this great effort.

Aware that there is not much time remaining, the Center-Left government of Premier Amintore Fanfani is working feverishly to formulate a master southern development plan. Though several cabinets had made a stab at something of the kind, as in the Vanoni Scheme of 1954, they were frustrated by the colossal amount of paper work and the monumental intricacies of the state bureaucracy. . . .

According to calculations made by the Cassa per il Mezzogiorno (Southern Fund), . . . [self-generating growth for the south by 1970] can be achieved by raising industrial production, lowering farm costs, and developing the kind of crops, processing, and marketing techniques best suited for the Common Market. Specifically, the goals are: to reduce the south's present agricultural force by one million in the next eight years—leaving only a quarter of its workers employed on the land—with half a million going north and the other half absorbed by new local industry; to create 1.5 million new nonagricultural jobs, so as to raise industrial production by 9.2 per cent a year; to further reduce unemployment by keeping children in school until the age of fourteen; and to double each farm worker's productivity so as to reach an annual average of $1,370, just under the present French level. All this will probably cost as much again in money and effort as southern reconstruction has cost up to now. It may succeed.

Whatever the weaknesses in the program so far, it has certainly made the south attractive for industrial investment. In the hands of various and often conflicting agencies—the Cassa, the Enti di Riforma (regional land-reform boards), the Consorzi Agrari (local reclamation committees), the ministries of agriculture, industry, health, education, and the budget—the work has been uncoordinated, frequently wasteful, and sometimes conspicuously shortsighted. The Taranto steel complex, for instance, will soon be using all the water that has been laboriously channeled to irrigate the outlying countryside, while the whole network of facilities to supply Bari's industrial zone—conduits, electric and telephone cables, roads, railroad sidings—is already inadequate for the factories being built there. But the fact that so many factories *are* being built there shows that the attraction exists. The question at this stage is where to find the capital for more.

A good deal of capital is ready to hand. Under the existing law, all state-owned industries in Italy, such as ENI (oil, gas, petrochemicals, fertilizer, rubber) and IRI (a tenth of the nation's industries, including shipbuilding and steel), must place 40 per cent of their investments in the south. Each has made immense contributions. For example, IRI has built the Taranto steel mill, which already has enough orders to pay for itself in record time, while ENI has put up a mammoth petrochemical plant in Gela, Sicily, and is constructing another near Matera to exploit the vast fields of natural gas it has found there. Between them, these groups have invested well over half a billion dollars in the south since 1959, and expect to spend three times as much by 1965.

Private capital has been following much more slowly. Until not long ago, almost any northern industrialist would have quailed at the idea of opening a factory in the south, where the trains were of nineteenth century vintage, the electric power (if available) often failed, the telephones were maddening, the local society hopelessly provincial, and the workers illiterate. But now they have learned to see the region as a good place for investment. For one thing, they have been getting along well for some time with these workers: half the north's labor force is southern. For another, the facilities are demonstrably improving. Where the government's efforts to create an industrial environment used to be dispersed, they are concentrated this year in four large "poles" and several smaller "areas" of development, the better to offer manufacturers every kind of service from fuel and transport to manpower training. Several big northern companies such as Montecatini, Ceramica Pozzo, and Olivetti have opened southern branches without calamity, and many others might be tempted.

Industrial congestion in the Milan-Turin-Bologna triangle has become so troublesome that the miracle has alrealy spread southward to most of central Italy—where the peasants can't be kept down on the farm, either—and there are quite a few attractions to lure it farther south. No region in Italy can match the south for cheap land, tax exemptions and rebates, concessions, write-offs, easy and generous government-backed loans, and a plentiful supply of labor. Added to that is the gradual realization that the southerners are picking up enough money to buy things, thus providing a useful outlet for industrialists anxious to reduce unit costs by expanding production, as Common Market competition requires.

All in all, therefore, the industrial outlook is promising. In agriculture, on the other hand, the going may be tougher. There the stakes are high indeed. The demand in the Common Market for many farm items—fruit, fats, oils—is already greater than the supply, and these are the things the south can produce best. But in Italy as a whole, the production derived from a dollar invested in agricultural labor can be equaled for 75 cents in France, 50 cents in Germany, 30 cents in Holland, and 17 cents in Belgium; and the south's yield is lower still. If productivity can be jacked up fairly quickly, there will be a bonanza. If not, there will be serious consequences in the Common Market and for all of Italy.

Agrarian experts have no illusions about a magic transformation. The south will need practically everything in massive quantities to improve its yield, including tractors and other farm machinery, fertilizer, better varieties of seed, more aqueducts and the water to fill them, modern refrigerating, canning, and shipping facilities—an over-all investment of something like $3.5 billion. The problem, however, isn't simply one of financing. While the south's feudal structure has vanished, the heritage lingers, especially among older peasants eternally suspicious of change; and while a social purpose may have been served in fracturing the great old estates into tiny fragments, the results are not always economically ideal. It will be a long while before millions of small landowners learn to alter their whole way of farming, and work successfully in cooperative teams.

Whether or not this can be done by 1970, or 1975—and whether or not Italy can find the money and strength to complete southern development by then—is still an open question. If the answer is "Yes," Italy's example will certainly be an inspiration for all those underdeveloped countries which have begun to doubt that a free society can redeem a seemingly doomed land without regimentation, forced labor, Stakhanovism, or iron dogma.

REBUILDING THE MEZZOGIORNO [5]

American industrialists have invested many millions of dollars in setting up new plants in Italy's underdeveloped south. One of the most recent is the heavy investment by Esso Standard Italiana for the construction of a factory for the production of high-quality selective lubricants, connected with its refinery of Rasiom near Augusta in Sicily. This will have a capacity of 200,000 tons a year and will be the largest such operation in Western Europe.

This American investment may be insignificant alongside the thousands of millions of lire which the Italian government has spent over the past eleven years in its endeavor to grapple with the problem of the *Mezzogiorno*—the economic situation of southern Italy, which starts twenty miles south of Rome and extends to the toe of Italy and to Sicily and Sardinia. But if the American capital invested is comparatively small it has stimulated others to take advantage of the special facilities granted by the government to set up factories in this area. This is especially so as the United States investment is often in collaboration with Italian firms.

[5] From "Italy's Troubled South," two articles by Walter Lucas, free-lance writer. *The Christian Science Monitor* (Eastern edition). p 17. Ap. 4, p 20. Ap. 5, '62. Reprinted by permission.

The problem of the *Mezzogiorno* is the most serious that successive Italian postwar governments have had to face. For here is a dead weight upon the whole of the national economy, even in this period of boom.

This has been obvious ever since Italy became one nation just one hundred years ago.

But it was not until 1950 that there was sufficient understanding of the problem, available finance, or the will to tackle Italy's underdeveloped areas in a major and imaginative way.

Stated simply the problem is: the *Mezzogiorno* covers 41 per cent of the national territory, houses 37 per cent of its population, and only contributes about 24 per cent of the total national income. The per capita income is very much lower than that of northern and central Italy. Unemployment and underemployment are chronic, and many parts of this area still are in a primitive economic state. . . .

To find a cure for this situation, the government of Signor Alcide de Gasperi set up in 1950 a special agency, the Cassa per il Mezzogiorno, to tackle the problem. This was allotted a sum of $1.6 billion to be spent over a ten-year period. Of this, 70 per cent was to go to agricultural improvements so as to increase the productivity of that economic sector and increase the standard of living of the bulk of the population in the south; 11 per cent was to be spent on such necessary adjuncts as aqueducts and irrigation; 9 per cent on roads; and 2.5 per cent on tourist facilities.

The basic idea behind this ten-year plan was to develop the natural resources, principally agricultural, and the aptitudes of the south. But at the same time the improvements to be brought in were to benefit the whole economy of the nation by strengthening the buying power of the population in that area; the finance, too, was to be raised from the country as a whole.

The plan, as well as the Cassa per il Mezzogiorno, was to be under the supervision of a special ministerial council; this was to be composed of the ministers for agriculture, public works, transport, treasury, trade and commerce, public health, social insurance, tourism, and state participations (this latter ministry was recently set up to control the growing participation of the state in the national economy). The composition of the council shows the breadth of the work which was to be undertaken.

Originally, though, only the intrastructures for agricultural development and improvement were to be set up—irrigation works, new housing, and subsidiary industries; but measures for a major plan of industrialization were not contemplated. It was thought at the time that a little stimulus to industrial activity would be enough to set the wheels of development in motion.

It soon became evident that if any real impression were to be made on the major problem of unemployment, or if the standards of living were to be brought anywhere near to those of the north, some attention must be paid to industrialization. Consequently, in 1952 the Cassa was authorized to raise large loans from abroad, a further $450 million was allocated by the government, and the plan was extended to twelve years. Most of this extra expenditure was to be devoted to the encouragement of private industrial enterprise.

But even with this expanded plan it was found in 1957 that the hoped-for results were not being achieved. At the same time Italy's economic boom was working wonders in northern and central Italy and permitted still more public money to be devoted to the development of the south. The plan was again revised, its term raised to fifteen years, and its funds were increased to an over-all $4 billion.

Seven years of experience had shown for one thing that an essential infrastructure both for agricultural and industrial development was better schools and provision for technical training. This, therefore, became a part of the new revised plan.

At the same time private enterprise was encouraged with the offer of special medium-term, low-interest-rate loans for the building of new factories in the south or the expansion or modernization of existing ones. Special attention was paid to the artisan, hotel, fishing, food processing and canning industries.

For this credit service three special financial organizations were set up, one dealing with the mainland, one with Sicily, and one with Sardinia.

Then the government passed a special law to induce foreign capital to invest in the south. Easy-term loans were offered, certain taxation exemptions were given, and it was made possible to transfer abroad capital, profits, and dividends.

To stimulate heavy industrial investment in the *Mezzogiorno*, the government also passed a law which compelled the state-controlled industries to place 40 per cent of their reinvestments and 60 per cent of their new investments in the south. Between 1957 and 1960 this involved a capital sum of $250 million.

For the next four years the state-owned corporations have an investment plan for the south which amounts to over $500 millions. This includes two major works: the steel mill at Taranto, one of the largest in Western Europe; and the refinery and petrochemical plants of ENI at Gela in Sicily.

All this public and private expenditure in southern Italy, Sicily, and Sardinia has involved wide measures of agricultural improvement, the division of land among the peasants, building new villages, the construction of roads and irrigation works, terracing of the mountainsides to prevent erosion, the encouraging of fruit canning and food processing, the institution of more cooperative methods of selling, specialized training in both agricultural and industrial techniques both for the worker and the managerial class, the setting up of industrial complexes in selected zones, the exploitation of the natural resources of the area where they exist—such as the important discovery of natural gas at Ferrandina, around which several industries have already grown.

Yet after all the money spent and the effort expended the results have been broadly disappointing.

II

Up to October 1961—that is, eleven years since the Cassa per il Mezzogiorno was instituted—about $2 billion of government funds and foreign loans have been spent in the development of southern Italy, Sicily, and Sardinia. That is just about half of the amount which has been allocated.

Of this sum 60 per cent has gone to agriculture in improving the productivity of this major national economic activity; out of the balance, $64 million has been spent on providing additional tourist facilities, $120 million has gone in easy, medium-term loans to 1,285 small industries. The rest has been spent on new schools and technical training institutions and all manner of financial inducements to large-scale industries, including those from abroad.

What have been the results of this vast expenditure of public money? To what degree has the major objective of narrowing the economic gap between the south and the rest of Italy been achieved?

On the face of it, the situation relatively has worsened. The percentage of the national income earned in the south has decreased, from about 24 per cent in 1958 to 22.69 per cent in 1960. This means that the economic disparity between the two Italies has widened even further.

However, in absolute terms the total income in the south has advanced from $3.1 billion in 1951 to $5.7 billion in 1960, or an increase of 80 per cent. The per capita income has risen from $180 to $310 during the same period, or an increase of 60 per cent.

Though this is an achievement, it still remains a fact that even after all the government effort the economic advance in northern and central Italy has been much more rapid than that in the south. . . .

In regard to unemployment, the situation in southern Italy certainly has improved. But this is primarily due to factors which have nothing to do with the government's development program. Over one million workers from the south have migrated to northern and central Italy over the past few years. They have been attracted by the magnet of full employment and higher wages than are to be found in the south.

It is interesting that while migration from the south is still a major feature of the way of things in that area, its direction has changed; it no longer goes overseas. The industrial boom in northern Italy has created a labor shortage, something that Italy has never before enjoyed. It is this shortage which is now being filled by those from the south who were previously accustomed to go abroad for work. . . .

There is, however, no reason to suppose that these migrants have been lost forever to the economy of the south; they are likely to drift back home again when the economic situation improves; in just the same manner as many Italians who emigrated to South America are now returning home because there are better opportunities for work and higher wages in Italy than in most of the South American countries.

It is obviously too early yet to draw any definite balance sheet on the results so far for the development plan for the *Mezzogiorno;* the effects of investment will only be seen in the long run, and efforts are still under way and being intensified to tackle this important national economic problem.

It is, however, possible to arrive at some conclusions now which are interesting not only for future Italian planning but for all those countries and international organizations which are faced with the same kind of problem and are trying to solve it. In fact this Italian experiment could well furnish a blueprint from which others could work.

From how things have gone, it is obvious that the Italian government did not fully appreciate the implications of the problem which they were tackling.

In the first place, it was not realized that in such a situation a plan concentrated principally on developing agricultural productivity could not attain the social and economic benefits sought.

Since the land, however improved, could not absorb the large numbers of surplus manpower (in fact modern methods of farming tend to put people off the land), any plan must be a coordination of agricultural and industrial development.

Then, too, it was not appreciated that better education and facilities for technical training both for workers and the managerial class were essential as a basis upon which to build agricultural and industrial development. These factors became evident after the plan had been in operation a few years, and were subsequently incorporated.

There are other considerations.

In the first place, large-scale industry, especially in the more modern types of manufacture, does not give employment in ratio to the capital invested. It was hoped that subsidiary industries would be stimulated and grow up around the large industrial complexes. As yet this has not happened.

A particular case in point has been seen in Sicily, where recent heavy industrialization near Augusta and Syracuse, which has involved large investments in refining, cement works, and petrochemical plants have not brought corresponding increase in employment. This is especially so here in similar areas, as such industries require qualified workers not to be found locally and often brought at great expense from northern Italy to satisfy the need.

This points to the importance of education as a part of a soundly based development plan, especially in an area like Italy's *Mezzogiorno,* where the incidence of illiteracy is high.

Then again, it has been shown that success can only be achieved if local enterprise is stimulated; too much dependence was placed on initiative from the north and from abroad, which is good as far as it goes, but it does not go far enough.

But more important still, it has been demonstrated that a problem of the magnitude and depth of the *Mezzogiorno* cannot be considered in isolation. It must be a part of a national economic plan.

It has become apparent from the experience of the past eleven years that as long as economic progress in northern and central Italy advances at so much greater pace than in the south the gap between the two Italies widens. The south may be better off than it was, but it still lags still further behind the other parts of the country and therefore remains a drag on the economy as a whole.

SAVING ITALY'S SOUTH [6]

At Rocca Imperiale in the Calabrian foothills half a dozen men were leaning against a wall in the shadow of Frederick II's great thirteenth century fortress. One of them pointed derisively at my camera.

"You think it's pretty here?" he shouted across to me. "Do you know that there's no water, and no sanitation? Tell them that in Rome. And tell them there soon won't be any people either. The village will be empty by the time the aqueduct gets here—already they can hardly find workmen to build it." His companions laughed.

Rocca Imperiale stands a few miles south of the Metaponto coastal plain, showpiece of Italy's postwar agricultural reform, and on the fringe of the area chosen by the Common Market Commission for its first experiment in regional planning. Twenty-five miles to the north, at Ferrandina, in the mountains of Lucania, the discovery of natural gas has brought in three firms to build petrochemical plants on the valley floor, and a motel is going up in an olive grove.

[6] From articles by a special correspondent to *The Times* (London). *The Times.* p 11. Jl. 11; p 11. Jl. 12, '63. Copyright by The Times. Reprinted by permission.

This is a typical corner of the *Mezzogiorno* today. Just when the government's postwar efforts to industrialize the poverty-stricken south are beginning to show results, the large-scale emigration which it hoped to avert has appeared. Some economists may welcome it, but the bitterness of the emigrants probably lay behind the Communist gains in the recent general election. The Center parties are afraid of what the Marxist Left may achieve in the next election if the outflow continues. . . .

A year ago . . . [the Brussels Commission] signed a contract with a Roman firm of planning consultants, Italconsult, to carry out studies for the promotion of an industrial "development pole," as it is called, in the provinces of Bari and Taranto. The idea is to survey existing industries and other assets in the region, work out in detail what type and quantity of further investment could turn it into a dynamic industrial complex, and then encourage the specific industries chosen to move to the spot.

It is a test case for the development pole idea, which is so fashionable nowadays. The question is whether selected points in an historically backward area like the Italian south can be brought without the assistance of tariff protection to the stage where they develop the capacity to grow unaided and keep abreast of modern industrial civilization. It is also a test case for the Common Market ideology, and for the Commission's planning powers, since harmonious regional development is a basic aim of the Rome Treaty [which established the Common Market].

From the start, the poverty of the *Mezzogiorno* was the biggest regional problem facing the Brussels Commission. The area includes the whole of the mainland south and east of Rome and the islands of Sicily and Sardina. It is the home of 19 million Italians, or two fifths of the total population, and accounts for over two fifths of the national territory. Italian nutritional experts say actual hunger has now been banished from the *Mezzogiorno*, even if many people's diets are still inadequate. But infant mortality was 53.8 a thousand on the southern mainland last year, compared with 31.2 in the north. . . . In 1961 personal consumption of goods and services was around . . . [$550] a head (already low by European standards) in the Milan-Turin-Genoa industrial region, while the figure for the *Mezzogiorno* was . . . [$302]. . . .

Apulia offered a number of advantages for the first development pole experiment. Bari had old-established trading connections in the eastern Mediterranean. It is often likened to Genoa, and gives a most unsouthern impression of orderly bustle. Brindisi has a fine harbor and is the second tourist port of Italy, though so far it has remained a point of transit. Taranto has some tradition of metalworking, thanks to the arsenal and naval dockyards, which used to employ 10,000 men.

Ferrandina lies in Matera province in Lucania, a byword for poverty and isolation, but its methane fields will soon be linked to Taranto by means of a *superstrada* (poor relation to a motorway) being driven down the Basento valley to join the fast Metaponto coast road. Much of the land in Apulia is rich, or potentially so, and produces for the market rather than for local consumption. Agricultural reform has gone well on the whole, and peasant poverty could be cured relatively easily by completing the irrigation projects and taking some of the weight of population off the land into local industry. Holdings could then be consolidated and mechanization extended.

The region is mostly flat, fairly homogeneous and well served by roads. Brindisi and Ferrandina balance each other on either side of the main Bari-Taranto axis, defining the development pole area, with Foggia also trying to industrialize in the middle of its rich agricultural tableland farther north. From Bari to Taranto is 62 miles, from Taranto to Brindisi 43 miles, from Brindisi to Bari 70 miles. Bari is the biggest town in Apulia, with 312,000 inhabitants, followed by Taranto (194,000), Foggia (118,000), Lecce (75,000) and Brindisi (70,000). Together they account for just under a quarter of Apulia's 3,300,000 inhabitants. Ferrandina is just a big hill village with 9,000 inhabitants.

The decision of the Italsider group to build Italy's biggest integrated steelworks at Taranto was Apulia's trump card when the development pole was chosen. This, and the Breda group's mechanical engineering projects at Bari, promised to provide a ready-made basis of heavy industry. Montecatini's choice of Brindisi as the site for a big petrochemical plant, and the natural gas at Ferrandina, were additional assets.

In the past two years each of these towns has acquired a raw industrial area where factories are rising rapidly out of agricultural land. Few of them are yet in production, but everywhere bulldozers are leveling, steel erectors are putting up the frames of the buildings, and contractors are finishing off compact housing estates for the workers. At Bari, Taranto, and Brindisi, the factories already under way will together give about 7,000 new jobs to each city—apart from the subsidiary employment created. The petrochemical plants in the Basento valley will employ 4,500 people from Ferrandina and other hill towns near by. At Foggia, four big food preserving and refrigerating plants are to be set up, and textile and building materials industries are also developing. All this may seem small beer but its impact is obvious in an area where little besides family-scale businesses had existed previously.

Three main factors account for this sudden flowering of industry after so many years of disappointment. One is a law passed in 1957 which obliged state-controlled enterprises to locate 60 per cent of all new investment in the *Mezzogiorno* up to 1965 (Italsider falls under this obligation as part of the IRI holding group, as does Breda and ENI, the state oil corporation). Another is the industrial areas law, also passed in 1957, which allows local consortia to expropriate suitable land and offer even greater inducements to private investors to build there than already existed. The third is the fact that the south, if it is still as far behind the north as ever, has now moved from subsistence into the bottom fringes of the market economy. The sprinkling of television aerials over the hill villages, the new electric cookers gleaming incongruously through medieval shop doorways in dusty, washing-hung streets, indicate that the *Mezzogiorno's* inhabitants are at last beginning to have enough purchasing power to interest businessmen.

II

The Italsider group's steelworks at Taranto represents industrialization on a scale never before dreamed of in this part of Italy. On the day I began my visit to the town there were three Russian freighters in port. They had come to load large-diameter steel pipes from the pipe mill which Italsider opened in advance of the main steelworks. The contract had been terminated under NATO pressure, but the mill was still carrying out an earlier phase of the contract.

There was room for only one freighter at a time at the pier. The other two were at anchor. Behind them, a line of dredgers and barges were fussing over a new two-mile-long breakwater already showing above the sea at one end. At the quayside below us, concrete caissons were being constructed for the new piers which Italsider is building to bring in its raw materials and export its steel.

Here was big business bursting through the seams of the old *Mezzogiorno.* An Italsider official explained that the government would pay for the new harbor eventually, but the company could not wait for the administrative processes to go through. It had set to work immediately at its own expense.

In the vast main hall of the pipe mill only a dozen workmen were to be seen. It looked like the luncheon break, but in fact the absence of men was due to automation. The production engineer said the mill was the twin of one in the United States. The Taranto workmen were regularly exceeding designed capacity by a few percentage points a week, while the Americans usually ran just below capacity. He thought a bonus scheme in Taranto might account for the higher productivity of the local men, many of whom had never seen a modern factory up to a few months ago.

Italsider's steelworks is to employ about 5,000 workmen and will have an annual output of 2 million tons initially. This will increase eventually to 6 million tons. Two other state-controlled companies, a cement works and a plant making refractories, are coming to the industrial area, together with a big Shell refinery, a beer bottling plant and a factory for structural steel. The biggest plant so far at Brindisi is Montecatini, employing about 4,000 men. Next comes its Polymer subsidiary with about 850 men, and a German small-diameter metal tube factory with about 500 employees. A factory using a Japanese process to produce food additive is expected, also with 500 employees.

All these projects together represent little more than a quarter of the new industry which Brindisi estimates it will need over the next decade or so to carry through its industrialization program. At Bari the main development is based on the Breda group's heavy and precision engineering plants, but [there are] two German [firms], one Swedish, one Finnish and one American (Coca-Cola) . . . building here.

Every factory manager I spoke to in Apulia said that local workers were at least as good as northerners. Some said they were better. As the managers were all from the north, the compliment meant something. Many northerners speak with contempt and even hostility of their southern fellow countrymen. They accuse them of a natural fecklessness and dishonesty which they see as sufficient explanation of their poverty. Often they view the government's development efforts as so much money wasted, at least until education changes the alleged character of the people. Fortunately, there are good historical reasons for the south's backwardness, more encouraging for the development planners. And if productivity is potentially as high in the south as in the north, wage costs can work out as much as 15 per cent lower here, since wage agreements in Italy are linked to each region's cost of living index. One way and another, Italconsult hopes its studies will prove convincingly that it is in the commercial interest of the required industries to move to the Bari-Taranto development pole.

Outside the main towns, much of Apulia is so closely cultivated as to resemble a rich market garden. Dessert grapes, olives, and almonds are the main traditional crops. The trouble is that too many people must live off each of these fertile orchards, and olives and almonds are not good subjects for mechanized farming. In the past year or two farm wages have jumped upwards, and thousands of smallholders are finding it uneconomic to employ men for the labor-intensive jobs of pruning and harvesting.

Originally the accent of agricultural reform, here as elsewhere in Italy, was on breaking up the big, underworked estates of the nobility and giving them in small lots to the landless men of the villages. Now the time is in sight when consolidation of smallholdings will be the order of the day, so that mechanized crops can be grown with highly paid, highly productive labor. It looks as if olive-growing must contract to the best orchards, and new crops will take over. Citrus fruits, for example, have been making rapid headway here since the war. The process of consolidation and mechanization should provide a steady labor reserve for industry for many years to come.

One of the key points of agricultural reform was to get the farmers out of their hill villages into farmhouses built on their holdings. Traditionally, everyone lived in the villages, no one in the valleys, which were haunts of malaria until a few years ago. Villages are often ten to fifteen miles apart, and walking or riding to the fields lying between means a huge wastage of man-hours. The system also makes livestock husbandry virtually impossible. However, many of the new farmhouses have no running water or light, and it is hard for an Italian to be cut off from the life of his native streets and squares, so the attempt at reform was only partly successful.

The hill villages are usually tortuous miles from the railways and highways in the valley, and many local people believe that they will eventually be abandoned. But they are cooler and airier than towns in the plains, and defended by ancient ties of history and habit. If the south succeeds in industrializing, many of the villages should find a happy future as compact dormitory towns or garden cities (almost all are surrounded by a belt of richly cultivated land, the kitchen gardens of the inhabitants), leaving the scenery and the good bottom land unencumbered.

Apulia and Lucania have a tourist potential which is only just being realized. In the past few years, development companies have suddenly bought up the most attractive parts of the endless white beaches stretching along the Metaponto coastline. The Adriatic coast is also beginning to waken up to its possibilities. Most of the foreign tourists come from Germany and France (the Germans have always been attracted by memories of Frederick II, whose castles dot the coastline), but the numbers are increasing rapidly. Each of the main towns already has more than one first-class hotel, and excellent restaurants.

Everyone I met in Apulia who was concerned with the development plans was confident that the region was at last getting started. The most sanguine, turning their backs on its humiliating slums, its lack of education, its heavy inheritance of inertia, saw a vision of a sort of new California, sunnier and less crowded than the north of the Common Market area, rich in tourists, and with modern growth industries exploiting its strategic position in the Mediterranean to capture the developing markets of Africa and the Middle East. After all, if Lombardy could prosper so far from the industrial heart of Europe in the Ruhr and southern England, why not Apulia?

In Rome people took a more guarded view, looking at cold statistics of gross investment and growth rates, and wondering whether Italy, her "miracle" apparently over, would not cripple herself with the effort of pulling the south up. However, the challenge is one for the EEC as well as for Italy. It is hard to say if they will succeed, but the *Mezzogiorno* today is certainly going somewhere.

BIBLIOGRAPHY

An asterisk (*) preceding a reference indicates that the article or a part of it has been reprinted in this book.

BOOKS, PAMPHLETS, AND DOCUMENTS

Adams, J. C. and Barile, Paolo. Government of republican Italy. Houghton. Boston. '61.

Albrecht-Carrié, René. Italy from Napoleon to Mussolini. Columbia University Press. New York. '60.

Allen, Edward. Merchants of menace: the Mafia. C. C. Thomas. Springfield, Ill. '62.

Ambrière, Francis, ed. Italy. Hastings. New York. '60.

Barbero, G. Land reform in Italy. (FAO Agricultural Studies no 53) Columbia University Press. International Documents Service. New York. '61.

Bayne, E. A. Italy's seeds of peril. (Southeast Europe Series X, no 1-5) American Universities Field Staff. Reports Service. 366 Madison Ave. New York 17. '62.

*Carey, J. P. C. and Carey, A. G. Italy—change and progress. (Headline Series no 158) Foreign Policy Association. 345 E. 46th St. New York 17. Mr.-Ap. '63.

Carlyle, Margaret. Awakening of southern Italy. Oxford University Press. New York. '62.

Carlyle, Margaret. Modern Italy. Rinehart. New York. '57.

Chase Manhattan Bank. New European market: a guide for American businessmen. The Bank. 1 Chase Manhattan Plaza. New York 15. '61.

Deakin, F. W. Brutal friendship: Mussolini, Hitler and the fall of Italian fascism. Harper. New York. '62.

Delzell, C. F. Mussolini's enemies. Princeton University Press. Princeton, N.J. '61.

Dolci, Danilo. Report from Palermo. Orion. New York. '59.

Duckett, E. S. Gateway to the middle ages. 3v. University of Michigan Press. Ann Arbor. '61.
Volume 1, Italy.

Einaudi, Mario and Goguel-Nyegaard, François. Christian Democracy in Italy and France. University of Notre Dame Press. South Bend, Ind. '52.

Gartler, M. Understanding Italy. Laidlaw. River Forest, Ill. '62.

Germino, Dante. Italian Fascist party in power. University of Minnesota Press. Minneapolis. '59.
Ginsburg, N. S. ed. Essays on geography and economic development. University of Chicago Press. Chicago. '60.
Grindrod, Muriel. Rebuilding of Italy. Royal Institute of International Affairs. London. '55.
Hildebrand, G. H. Stability and growth in the postwar Italian economy. New York State School of Industrial and Labor Relations. Cornell University. Ithaca, N.Y. '61.
Horowitz, Daniel. Italian labor movement. Harvard University Press. Cambridge, Mass. '63.
Hostetter, Richard. Italian Socialist movement. Van Nostrand. Princeton, N.J. '58.
Hughes, H. S. United States and Italy. Harvard University Press. Cambridge, Mass. '53.
Italian Embassy. Commercial Office. Italy: an economic profile 1962. The Embassy. 2401 15th St. Washington 9, D.C. Je. '63.
Italian Information Center. Italy's general elections. The Center. 686 Park Ave. New York 21. '63.
Part I—Background; Part II—Complete returns; New Parliament.
Italian Society for International Organization. Italy and the United Nations. Manhattan Publishing Company. New York. '59.
Jemolo, A. C. Church and state in Italy. Dufour. Philadelphia. '61.
Kogan, Norman. Government of Italy. Crowell. New York. '62.
Kogan, Norman. Politics of Italian foreign policy. Praeger. New York. '63.
Kubly, Herbert. American in Italy. Simon and Schuster. New York. '55.
Kubly, Herbert. Italy. (Life World Library) Time. New York. '61.
Lampedusa, G. T. The leopard. Pantheon. New York. '60.
Levi, Carlo. Christ stopped at Eboli. Farrar, Straus. New York. '47.
Levine, I. R. Main Street, Italy. Doubleday. Garden City, N.Y. '63.
Lutz, Vera. Italy: a study in economic development. Oxford University Press. New York. '63.
McCarthy, Mary. Stones of Florence. Harcourt. New York. '59.
McCarthy, Mary. Venice observed. Reynal. New York. '56.
Mack Smith, Denis. Italy; a modern history. University of Michigan Press. Ann Arbor. '59.
Maxwell, Gavin Ten pains of death. Dutton. New York. '60.
Morris, James. World of Venice. Pantheon. New York. '60.
Neufeld, M. F. Italian past and the future of impoverished nations. New York State School of Industrial and Labor Relations. Cornell University. Ithaca, N.Y. '63.
Olschki, Leonardo. Genius of Italy. Cornell University Press. Ithaca, N.Y. '54.

Ottieri, Ottiero. Men at the gate. Houghton. Boston. '62.
Ottieri, Ottiero and Colombo, Furio. Two Italian visitors. (Report no 289) Yale Reports. Woodbridge Hall. Yale University. New Haven, Conn. '63.
Pan American World Airways. Complete reference guide to Italy and its islands. The Airways. New York. '63.
Salomone, A. W. Italy in the Giolittian era: Italian democracy in the making, 1900-1914. University of Pennsylvania Press. Philadelphia. '60.
Sorbello, U. di, comp. Italy: a brief outline. Italian Embassy. Cultural Division. 686 Park Ave. New York 21. n.d.
United States. Department of Commerce. Basic data on the economy of Italy. E. F. Mullelly. (Economic Reports no 62-51) Supt. of Docs. Washington 25, D.C. Je. '62.
United States. Department of Commerce. Bureau of International Commerce. Economic development in Italy, 1962. (Overseas Business Reports) Supt. of Docs. Washington 25, D.C. Mr. '63.
Webster, R. A. The cross and the fasces: Christian Democracy and fascism in Italy. Stanford University Press. Stanford, Calif. '60.
Wendt, P. F. Post World War II housing policies in Italy. (Reprint no 31) University of California. Institute of Business and Economic Research. Real Estate Research Program. Berkeley. '62.

PERIODICALS

America. 108:395-6. Mr. 23, '63. Pope John: new look. Philip Land.
America. 108:405-6. Mr. 23, '63. Adzhubei and Italy today. Martin Painelle.
America. 108:712-13. My. 18, '63. Elections in Italy. Martin Painelle.
American Economic Review. 51:390-9+. My. '61. Growth and stability in the postwar Italian economy. G. H. Hildebrand.
Atlantic. 206:20+. S. '60. Atlantic report.
Atlantic. 210:24-31. S. '62. Atlantic report.
Atlas. 4:172-82. S. '62. Fig leaves and politics. M. Argentieri and I. Cifriani.
Atlas. 4:194-209. S. '62. Power octopus: Italy's oil and gas monopoly exposed. Indro Montanelli.
Atlas. 6:328-51. D. '63. Neo-Risorgimento.
Banco di Roma Review of Economic Conditions in Italy. Jl. '63. Italian economy: 1962.
Business Week. p 112-14. F. 24, '62. In Italy, boom of the '50s just keeps on rolling.
Business Week. p 148-50+. F. 23, '63. Italy bids to rule the waves.
Business Week. p 114. Ag. 17, '63. Italy: stability and inflation fight it out.

Catholic World. 197:372-9. S. '63. Italy: problem for Pope Paul.
Challenge. 10:24-7. Ap. '62. ENI: Italy's economic colossus. Joachim Joesten.
Christian Century. 79:359-60. Mr. 21, '62. Letter from Italy. G. A. Leiper.
*Christian Science Monitor (Eastern edition). p 13. Mr. 23, '61. Italy: a quiet success. J. G. Harrison.
*Christian Science Monitor. p 17. Ap. 4; p 20. Ap. 5, '62. Italy's troubled south. Walter Lucas.
Christian Science Monitor. p 10. My. 14, '62. Italy: on the way up. Walter Lucas.
*Christian Science Monitor. p 12. Je. 13, '62. Italy faces inflation threat. Walter Lucas.
Christian Science Monitor. p 1C. Je. 25, '62. Mistrust splits south Tyrol. Ernest Pisko.
Christian Science Monitor. p 5B. Ja. 16, '63. Leveling seen in Italy's rising economy. Walter Lucas.
*Christian Science Monitor. p 19. Mr. 29, '63. Supermarkets dent Italian food costs. Keith de Folo.
Christian Science Monitor. p 15. Ap. 11, '63. Growth rate slows in Italy. Walter Lucas.
Christian Science Monitor. p 13. Ap. 18, '63. Credit buying spreads in Italy. Walter Lucas.
Christian Science Monitor. p 11. Ap. 24, '63. Italy relaxes law on overseas marts. Walter Lucas.
*Christian Science Monitor. p 11. My. 2, '63. Youth boost Italian Reds. Mario Rossi.
*Christian Science Monitor. p 1C. My. 7, '63. EEC tests Italian agriculture. Walter Lucas.
Christian Science Monitor. p 17. My. 10, '63. Southern Italy balks economists. Walter Lucas.
Christian Science Monitor. p 11. Je. 4, '63. Italian trends analyzed. Walter Lucas.
Christian Science Monitor. p 2. Jl. 13, '63. Rome grips bulging seams. Walter Lucas.
Commentary. 31:119-26. F. '61. Danilo Dolci: non-violence in Italy. Kathleen Nott.
Commonweal. 72:125-6. Ap. 20, '60. Soul of Sicily. G. D. Kumlien.
Commonweal. 73:196-7. N. 18, '60. Two Italies, north and south. J. J. Navone.
Commonweal. 74:225-6. My. 26, '61. Roman irony. G. D. Kumlien.
Commonweal. 76:391-3. Jl. 13, '62. Italy's new look: Christian Democrats and the Left.
Commonweal. 77:639-41. Mr. 15, '63. Fellini's La dolce Italia. J. J. Navone.

Commonweal. 78:244-5. My. 24, '63. Trend to the Left. G. D. Kumlien.

Contemporary Review. 202:10-14. Jl. '62. Italian predicament. Axel Heyst.

Contemporary Review. 204:29-32. Jl. '63. Italy after the election. Axel Heyst.

Current History. 40:1-52. Ja. '61. West Europe and continuing coexistence.
Italy: a century of unity. W. C. Askew. p 34-9.

Current History. 42:154-9. Mr. '62. Italian economy: chiaroscuro. Massimo Salvadori.

Dun's Review. 79:55. My. '62. Fiat—Italian giant and "workers' paradise."

Economist. 197:340-1. O. 22, '60. Italy in two centuries.

Economist. 198:251. Ja. 21, '61. Agricultural perplexities in Italy.

*Economist. 200:48-9. Jl. 1, '61. Italian labour out of step.

Economist. 201:658+. N. 18, '61. Italian Communists in disarray.

Economist. 204:704-5. Ag. 25, '62. Feudal fish in Sardinia.

Economist. 204:1115. S. 22, '62. Fresh markets for Italian wines.

Economist. 205:133-4. O. 13, '62. Clash over Latin in Italy.

Economist. 207:688. My. 18, '63. Italy's Mezzogiorno: a verdict on the good fairy.

*Editorial Research Reports. 1:179-83. Mr. 6, '63. Italian politics and elections. Jeanne Kuebler.

*Encounter. 18:7-17. Je. '62. Difference in the south. Luigi Barzini.

Esquire. 55:84-6. F. '61. Italy. E. Hughes.

Foreign Affairs. 39:221-39. Ja. '61. Italy after one hundred years. C. B. Luce.

Foreign Affairs. 40:213-23. Ja. '62. Where the Italian Socialists stand. Pietro Nenni.

Fortune. 63:77-8. F. '61. New Renaissance.

*Fortune. 66:96-101+. D. '62. New Italian managers. Spencer Klaw.

Fortune. 67:53-5+. My. '63. The Mezzogiorno. Robert Neville.

Fortune. 68:102-7. Ag. '63. Half-billion-dollar lace to tie the Italian boot.

Harper's Magazine. 222:79-85. Mr. '61. Italy's new Caesar. Robert Neville.

Harper's Magazine. 226:26+. Ap. '63. Mediterranean mosaic. Herbert Mitgang.

Holiday. 29:11-17. Mr. '61. Party of one. Aubrey Menen.

Holiday. 30:26-39. Ag. '61. Milan: city of the golden touch. Aubrey Menen.

Holiday. 30:80-5+. N. '61. Sad and beautiful is land of Sicily. Alan Moorehead.

Holiday. 31:38-49+. Je. '62. Italy's smiling coast. Aubrey Menen.

Holiday. 33:50-1+. Ja. '63. Journey along the Po. Eric Newby.
Horizon. 4:20-45. S. '61. Sicily. M. I. Finley and Denis Mack Smith.
Horizon. 4:120-8. N. '61. La dolce via. J. M. Fitch.
Italian Affairs. 11:3831-43. Mr.-Ap. '62. Economic situation in Italy.
Italian Affairs. 12:4237-40. Ja.-F. '63. Growth of industry and commerce in the past ten years.
Journal of Commerce. Sec. 2, p 1-8+. Ap. 18, '63. Era of Italian industrial progress.
Journal of Commerce. p 10. Jl. 24, '63. Italian economy held strengthening. N. LoBello.
Life International. 30:47+. Je. 5, '61. North Italy's boom. Herbert Kubly.
Listener. 67:5-7. Ja. 4, '62. The Mafia. Denis Mack Smith.
Listener. 70:10-13. Jl. 4, '63. Good-natured Milan. Ian Nairn.
Nation. 196:327-9. Ap. 20, '63. Italy: a new village around an old fountain. E. M. Borgese.
National Geographic Magazine. 119:542-69. Ap. '61. Venice. J. A. Morris.
National Geographic Magazine. 120:593-648. N. '61. United Italy marks 100th year. N. T. Kennedy.
National Geographic Magazine. 123:743-89. Je. '63. Italian Riviera, land that winter forgot. Howell Walker.
National Review. 11:338. N. 18, '61. Italian conservatives. Russell Kirk.
National Review. 14:404-5. My. 21, '63. Signor Fanfani's self-made bed. Alice Leone-Moats.
National Review. 15:152-3. Ag. 27, '63. Will Italian democracy survive? David Futch.
New Leader. 44:10-12. Ja. 2, '61. Blow-up over Tyrol. V. Tortora.
New Leader. 44:9-10. My. 1, '61. Italy's economic miracle. Walter Lucas.
New Leader. 45:6-8. Mr. 5, '62. Italy opens to the Left. Mauro Calamandrei.
*New Leader. 45:24-6. D. 10, '62. Italy and mass culture. Raymond Rosenthal.
New Leader. 46:14-16. Ja. 7, '63. In Italy. Mauro Calamandrei.
*New Leader. 46:14-15. My. 27, '63. Understanding Italy's vote. Mauro Calamandrei.
New Republic. 144:9-10. Je. 12, '61. Italy and the new frontier. L. J. Wollemborg.
New Republic. 146:10-11. Ja. 29, '62. Isolating the Communists. L. J. Wollemborg.
New Republic. 147:10-12. S. 10, '62. New frontier and the new Italy. L. J. Wollemborg.

New Statesman. 65:789-90. My. 24, '63. Togliatti speaks his mind. K. S. Karol.
New Statesman. 65:858+. Je. 7, '63. Red Bologna. Richard West.
*New York Times. p 1+. S. 18, '61. Italy enters the age of affluence but continues to battle poverty. E. L. Dale, Jr.
*New York Times. p 30. Ag. 15, '62. Italy starts to unify at last. C. L. Sulzberger.
New York Times. p 4. S. 14, '62. Many Italians question effect of program to develop south. Arnaldo Cortesi.
New York Times. p 45. Ap. 19, '63. Inflation brings added pressure. L. E. Magnani.
New York Times. p 45+. Ap. 19, '63. Investors hold key to providing Italy with a needed spur. Arnaldo Cortesi.
New York Times. p 36. My. 1, '63. Communist gain in Italy.
New York Times. p 12F. My. 26, '63. South Italy leaps centuries in drive for modern industry.
*New York Times. p 22. Ag. 9, '63. Another "catastrophic perspective"? C. L. Sulzberger.
New York Times. p 12. O. 30, '63. Italian Socialists back move to join coalition. Arnaldo Cortesi.
New York Times Magazine. p 39+. N. 5, '61. Roman paradox: la rossa vita. Paul Hofmann.
*New York Times Magazine. p 40+. F. 18, '62. "La bella Italia"—myths and truths. Joan Marble [Cook].
New York Times Magazine. p 79+. Mr. 18, '62. La dolce vita sans kissing. Robert Neville.
New York Times Magazine. p 22+. Ap. 29, '62. Antiques and antics in Italy. Paul Hofmann.
*New York Times Magazine. p 32+. My. 26, '63. Italy's intellectuals steer to the Left. Joan Marble Cook.
*New York Times Magazine. p 12+. Je. 2, '63. Catholic—yet Communist—why? Robert Neville.
New Yorker. 38:128+. S. 8, '62. Letter from Milan. William Murray.
Newsweek. 58:66-8. Jl. 10, '61. Rebirth in Italy; three great movie directors. C. G. Pepper.
Newsweek. 59:78-9+. F. 19, '62. Italy's state within a state—the empire run by Enrico Mattei.
Newsweek. 60:80+. N. 12, '62. Choice for ENI.
Orbis. 5:411-24. Winter '62. Trends in Italy: an "Opening to the Left?" Ernesto De Marchi.
Political Quarterly. 34:185-93. Ap. '63. Italy in transition. Ninetta Jucker.
*Progressive. 27:25-8. Ag. '63. Italy's haunted south. Gabriel Gersh.
Quarterly Journal of Economics. 76:515-47. N. '62. Development policies for southern Italy. H. B. Chenery.

Reader's Digest. 80:158-9+. F. '62. Awakening in the Tuscan hills. Robert Littell.

*Reporter. 25:34-6. Jl. 6, '61. Lost decades in Italian history. Claire Sterling.

Reporter. 25:43-4+. N. 9, '61. Few hours in Narni, Orvieto, Avezzo. R. M. Coates.

*Reporter. 26:22-6. Ja. 4, '62. Communist roadblock in Italian politics. Claire Sterling.

Reporter. 26:15+. My. 24, '62. Italy's new president.

*Reporter. 27:32-4. S. 27, '62. Transformation south of Rome. Claire Sterling.

*Reporter. 28:22-5. My. 23, '63. Italian elections: even worse than before. Claire Sterling.

*St. Louis Post-Dispatch. p 1D+. Ap. 17, '63. Confident Italy expects economy to keep on growing. T. W. Ottenad.

*Saturday Review. 44:19-55. F. 11, '61. One hundred years of Italy. Katharine Kuh and Sergio Pacifici, eds.

Reprinted in this book: Sense of rapture. John Ciardi. p 20-3+; Puzzle of history. H. S. Hughes. p 26-8.

Senior Scholastic. 82:14-17. My. 1, '63. Italy's postwar economic miracle.

Spectator. 210:485. Ap. 19, '63. Election in Umbria. Michael Adams.

Spectator. 211:201. Ag. 16, '63. Rome relaxed. Kate O'Brien.

Statist. 178:382-3. N. 9, '62. Successor for Mattei. Giorgio Borsa.

Swiss Review of World Affairs. 12:7-8. Ja. '63. Italy's controversial economic order. C. Motteli.

Swiss Review of World Affairs. 13:5-9. Ap. '63. Italy on the eve of parliamentary elections. Hans Tutsch.

Swiss Review of World Affairs. 13:3-4. Je. '63. Italy's *democrazia cristiana* at a crossroads. Hans Tutsch.

Texas Quarterly. 4:7-267. Summer '61. Image of Italy. W. Arrowsmith, ed.

Think. 29:18-22. My.-Je. '63. Made in Italy, sold everywhere. Richard Wilcox.

Time. 76:25. Ag. 15, '60. In darkest southern Europe.

Time. 77:24. Je. 23, '61. Trouble in Tyrol.

Time. 78:66+. Jl. 21, '61. State within a state.

*Time. 79:72-9. Ja. 12, '62. Italy's booming north.

Time. 81:88+. Mr. 29, '63. Dream of domination: state-owned Italian Line.

Times (London). p 15. Je. 29; p 13. Je. 30, '60. Kingdom of the two Sicilies.

*Times (London). p 11. Jl. 11; p 11. Jl. 12, '63. Saving Italy's south.

Vogue. 137:164+. Mr. 1, '61. Italy—a living summary of all history. Carlo Levi.

Vogue. 141:106-9. Ap. 15, '63. Sardinia.

Wall Street Journal. p 8. My. 29, '61. South Italy is floundering economically despite billions spent through planning. Dan Cordtz.

Wall Street Journal. p 1+. Jl. 30, '62. Uneasy Italy. Ray Vicker.

Washington Post. p K1-K9. Ag. 19, '62. Dynamic Italy.

Washington Post. p A26. D. 17, '62. Italian industries migrate south. Ninetta Jucker.

Washington Post. p E7. Ap. 7, '63. Italy tailors its high schools. L. J. Wollemborg.

Washington Post. p A15. My. 15, '63. Living cost is cited in Red gains. L. J. Wollemborg.

World Today. 18:23-9. Ja. '62. De-Stalinization in the Italian Communist party. Sylvia Sprigge.

Yale Review. 50:491-503. Je. '61. Reflections on a centennial: the Italian Risorgimento. T. G. Bergin.